Christian George w ... es by the bucket-loads, ar ... nd Reformation, Puritan ... d- vice from saints in eve... ed with the urgency and joy of spiritual disci... age often employed) for the soul.

Tom J. Nettles
Professor of historical theology
The Southern Baptist Theological Seminary

• • •

Christian George's paragraphs are like a good clean mirror, showing us who we are. And finding out who we are is step one in the journey of becoming who we want to be.

For some time I have been his friend. In more recent days I have been his professor. Lately I have been his mentee, and reading his books is like reading his life—it has left me a debtor to his discipline, his walk of faith, and his candor.

Calvin Miller
Author of The Singer *Trilogy*

• • •

Christian George is one of an emerging generation of young leaders who can speak in a language that young evangelicals will access. He does it from a solidly biblical base, and writes with power and clarity. In *Godology* he helps readers better understand God's transcendence as well as the tension between human freedom and divine sovereignty. His straight talk approach may rattle a few readers. But I welcome his continuing contributions to reaching the next generation of leaders.

Chuck Colson
Author, The Faith
Founder, Prison Fellowship

• • •

Christian George strings words together like a spider spins a web. It's easy to get caught up in what he's doing, and what he's doing is great—simultaneously clearing away confusion and embracing the mystery of a God who is beyond us and yet with us. *Godology* is a created word—much like each of us, I suppose—that carries great weight.

David Zimmerman
author, Deliver Us from Me-Ville

Christian George has a beautiful way of drawing us into some of the most profound and nourishing mysteries of the Christian faith. He's funny. He's a lively and engaging writer and he's honestly hopeful that God is transforming our lives and the world. He woos us with wit, vulnerability, and passion into the gospel's "swirling narrative of blood and forgiveness."

Debbie Blue
Author, From Stone to Living Word

• • •

Christian George uses fresh, contemporary language to call Christians into a deeper relationship with God through countercultural spiritual disciplines. Heeding his words may be painful but will surely help us delight more in Jesus Christ and worry less about ourselves.

Collin Hansen
Author, Young, Restless, Reformed

• • •

Godology is a trustworthy title for George's compendium on approaching God. Written in a readable, breezy style, the book will hold the attention of youth, and as a senior citizen I found it helpful (as a young-in-heart) in identifying with young people. I have longed and prayed for unity among believers in all God's people, and George has helped me make an unexpected step toward unity with all ages. All Christians, young and old, should read this book.

T. W. Hunt
Author of The Doctrine of Prayer *and* The Mind of Christ

God·ol·o·gy

God·ol·o·gy

\god-ä-lə-jē\
noun

1 because knowing God changes everything

CHRISTIAN GEORGE

moody publishers
chicago

Editor: Jim Vincent
Cover design: Brand Navigation
Interior design: Smartt Guys design

Library of Congress Cataloging-in-Publication Data

George, Christian Timothy, 1981-
Godology : because knowing God changes everything / Christian George.
p. cm.
ISBN 978-0-8024-8255-6
1. God (Christianity)--Attributes--Meditations. 2. Spiritual life--Christianity. I. Title.
BT130.G46 2009
231'.4--dc22

2008036330

This book is printed on acid free recycled paper containing 30% PCW (Post Consumer Waste) and manufactured in the United States of America by Bethany Press.

We hope you enjoy this book from Moody Publishers. Our goal is to provide high-quality, thought-provoking books and products that connect truth to your real needs and challenges. For more information on other books and products written and produced from a biblical perspective, go to www.moodypublishers.com or write to:

Moody Publishers
820 N. LaSalle Boulevard
Chicago, IL 60610

1 3 5 7 9 10 8 6 4 2

Printed in the United States of America

For my mom

Con•tents

Fore•word

In a bright, brave, boisterous rush, Christian George here deftly clothes eternal truths about God and godliness in twenty-first-century street-cred attire. What he says is classic mainstream theology, echoing and reinforcing the clear and consistent teaching of the Bible, but the way he says it freshens it with sometimes startling effect.

His expositions sting and stimulate simultaneously, in the manner of Tabasco sauce. Tabasco, of course, though loved by great numbers, is not to everyone's taste; some say that it actually spoils the food. So it may be a few will wince at George's quick-fire, whiz-bang style and feel it goes over the top, undermining reverence for the sake of shock effect. To which, in our age of multiple literary subcultures, the best response may be that the title *Godology* gives fair warning of what is to come, and if you are not going to appreciate George's semi-pop idiom, you had best conclude straightaway that this book is not for you. (It is actually for older teens and twentysomethings, for whom the pop singer's idiom is familiar ground, but its contemporary beat will strike chords with older readers as well.)

The bottom line for George is the prime importance of knowing God. That is so for me, too, though I belong to an older generation that writes a more sober-sided English. But I applaud this book for its purpose and content, and commend it enthusiastically to those for whom it is designed, and with whom it will surely ring bells.

By writing *Godology*, Christian George has rendered significant service for the good of souls and the glory of God.

J. I. PACKER

Author of *Knowing God*

Board of Governors professor of theology, Regent College

"Yeah, I went hunting once. Shot a deer in the leg.
Had to kill it with a shovel.
Took about an hour. Why do you ask?"

—*Michael Scott,* The Office

Introduction

Rakes for Shovels

• • •

\ˈshə-vəls\

Since I can't afford my own Brookstone vibrating massage chair, I often go to the mall to use theirs. It's a shameless way to spend a Saturday, but the payoff is enormous. One day as waves of glory saturated my shoulders, a young girl approached the chair. She waited for her turn and gave me some serious eye attitude. I pretended not to see her as mechanical fingers kneaded my grateful glutes.

"Ahem!" she fake-coughed.

Normally I would be a gentleman and surrender such a seat, but suddenly the chair switched gears and started on my calves. "*Thank You, Jesus!*" It was a heavenly moment and I wasn't about to come back down to earth. Two minutes later, the whiny girl was dragged away by her mom, but not without leaving me with the Preadolescent Glare of Death.

Our culture tells us to take care of our bodies. We feed them, massage them, shave them, and bathe them. We don't think twice about dropping a hundred bucks here and there on whatever makes us healthier or more comfortable.

But what about our souls? Our stomachs are full, but our souls are starving. Jesus said, "It takes more than bread to really live" (Luke 4:4). It takes discipline. It takes a desire to burn off spiritual cellulite and feast upon the energizing presence of God.

Not too long ago, I googled *God*. Turns out, there were five hundred sixty-four million results. As I waded through the first page, I came to the conclusion that everyone has an opinion about God. This world is full of those who think about Him, from the animal-worshipping tribesman to the humming monk in Asia. Even Amazon lists half a million books in print on the subject. So do we really need another book about God?

I think so. J. I. Packer once said that Christianity in America is three thousand miles wide and one inch deep. Our faith has been fossilized too long. We need to go deeper. We're on the verge of an awakening, trading a kiddy pool Christianity for the deep things of God. It's time to crank up the bulldozer—bone marrow awaits! We are wading out of the creeks and into the depths. No more treading water. With scuba tanks and weight belts, we're plunging into the Scriptures to find treasure beyond imagination. It takes a radical faith to plumb a bottomless God, and we're ready for the odyssey.

A. W. Tozer said, "What comes into our minds when we think about God is the most important thing about us."[1] In a world created by God, sustained by God, and renewed by God, nothing is more important than knowing God.

We are ready for a revolution. As Eugene Peterson wrote in *The Message*, "Ignorance of God is a luxury you can't afford in times like these" (1 Corinthians 15:34). It only takes a spark to ignite a country, and God is pouring diesel on His people. God isn't as calm or tame as we thought. He bursts from the Tupperware we seal Him in, and He's on the move. He's calling us to wipe off our spiritual milk mustaches, exchange earthly habits for holy ones, and gorge ourselves on the nourishing Bread of Life.

Since Christianity is an upward, inward, and outward faith, each chapter in this book explores a facet of God, a spiritual discipline, and a practical expression of that truth. In a time when *discipline* sounds like a four-letter word, these responses to God's nature will help us know Him up close and personally.

- Prayer
- Obedience
- Art
- Journaling
- Silence
- Fasting
- Vow Making
- Meditation
- Solitude
- Labyrinth Walking
- Practicing God's Presence

It's impossible to condense God into a book—no one can really inventory the Eternal. But *Godology* is my attempt to dive into the mysteries of God. As you read this book, hold it up to the light of the Bible and see if God is as great as you think He might be.

This isn't a safe read, but then again, God isn't a safe God.[2] So exchange your rake for a shovel and let's see what lies beneath the surface.

"And I will travel to New Zealand.
And walk the Lord of the Rings trail to Mordor."

—*Dwight Schrute,* The Office

1

Mardi Gras and Icicles

• • •

God's Unity \ˈyōōn-ə-tē\

So I'm standing on a parade route in New Orleans yelling my head off for beads. It's Mardi Gras and electricity zigzags through the air. The jazz is swinging, the floats are rolling, and I'm dancing like the world's about to end. To my regret, I catch a glimpse of a topless fat guy catching doubloons. On his belly is a bright red fleur de lis, the official emblem of New Orleans. The petals wiggle as if independent from his body. I wince—no wonder they call it "Fat Tuesday."

The next Sunday I stumble into church. A general boredom seems to hang over the congregation. As the music plays, I don't feel like getting my praise on. My hands won't clap. My feet won't dance. I try to squeal out a few notes, but my throat is hoarse. I face the truth: I'm all used up—just another dehydrated Christian sucked dry by the fangs of worldliness.

• • •

The Trinity is a mystery. No doubt about it. But this is what we know: God has forever existed in three persons—Father, Son, and Spirit. Before cities were constructed or worlds created, God hung out with Himself. He was His own party. Some say three's a crowd, but in this VIP club, the King, Prince, and Advocate General share a perfect blend of intimacy, community, and eternity.

How can God be one and three at the same time? Got me. Reminds me of the day at a thrift store when I stumbled upon a faded blue Bruce Lee T-shirt. Lee was really laying down the law with a flying dragon kick. The shirt didn't have any bloodstains, so I decided to try it on. As I stepped into the three-way mirror, a thousand kung fu kicks appeared in the distance. Each pane of glass reflected the images of the others. And I stood in awe, gazing at the Bruce Lee infinity.

I'm still trying to figure out how Bruce Lee jumped that high. But I've given up trying to figure out how God can be one and three at the same time. The English language can't articulate the unity of God. Though grammatically troubling, it's perfectly accurate to say that God are one and They is three.[1] Like a three-way mirror, each person in the Godhead satellites the other—an eternal reflection—forever bright, forever burning, forever dressed in glory. Most families have some degree of dysfunction, but not God. In Him there is no distant stepfather, prodigal son, or absentee spirit.

Believe it or not, the word *Trinity* is actually not written in the Bible.[2] But the Scriptures clearly teach the unity of God: "Hear, O Israel: The Lord our God, the Lord is one" (Deuteronomy 6:4). They also teach the diversity of God: "Therefore go and make disciples of all nations, baptizing them in the name of the Father and of the Son and of the Holy Spirit" (Matthew 28:19). So we believe them both.

One of the few advantages of living in a postmodern era is that people don't need a cold scientific explanation to believe in the supernatural anymore. Modernism is behind us. In the eighteenth century the Age of Faith gave way to an Age of Reason. But now in the twenty-first century, we are entering into another great Age of Faith. Because of our emphasis on experience, relationships, and story, postmoderns are primed to accept a faith that is wrapped in God's story, clothed in personal experience, and built on a solid, personal relationship with Christ. Because we are living in an age of mystery, we can appreciate what we can't fully understand about God.

We understand the Trinity as much as ants understand airplanes.

We are living in an age when we know that the more we know, the more we know that we don't know much at all. You know? And such knowledge makes us small again.

The fleur de lis that wiggled on the belly of the New Orleans doubloon catcher has a noble tradition. Throughout history, it has appeared on European coats of arms, flags, logos, and decorations. It's always been a symbol of the Trinity, each petal representing a person in the Godhead. Like the Irish three-leafed clover, symbols like these help us bend our brains around God's mysteries. Like a mind, God is intellect, memory, and will—one system, but three functions.[3] Like water, God is fluid, steam, and icicle—one substance, but three textures. These pictures can be powerful, but eventually they melt down and cannot illustrate the infinite essence of God.

We understand the Trinity as much as ants understand airplanes—it's way over our heads. We embrace the mystery of the Trinity because it has embraced us. Christ has taken note of our smallness, our gritty frailness, and He loves us three-dimensionally.

In God's global positioning system, our location is triangulated. Christians are drawn by the Father (John 6:44), saved by the Son (John 3:16), and sealed by the Holy Spirit (Ephesians 4:30). Nothing can scramble what God has secured.

Returning to Two Knees

Because we are made in God's image, we have the ability to speak. Our tongues communicate what our minds originate. And though we are masters of chitchat, we crave connection, connection to each other, to the Internet, to information that affects our decisions, and ultimately to the God who spoke us into being.

Christianity is not about God making bad people good. It's about God making dead corpses live.[4] And how do living creatures pray? Sometimes with words . . . "Now I lay me down to sleep, I pray the Lord my soul to keep." Sometimes with sighs . . . a tired "uhhggg" after a long day of work. But most of the time we pray with thoughts—at a stoplight, on a lunch break, beneath the weight bar during a workout. These are passing prayers—random requests—but God hears all of them. Why? Because God created us for conversation. He installed a modem inside every heart with a direct line to divinity. We have real-time access to His ear. And if we believe that God is truly with us, in every room, at every moment, prayer becomes less an activity and more an attitude. It's our meat and potatoes. It's the umbilical cord connecting us to Christ.

Babies spend a lot of time on their knees. They crawl, roll, and drool on themselves. But when babies grow older, they learn to stand up. They learn to walk, jog, and skip. They jump on trampolines and run through parks. But the taller we grow, the more we need to return to our two knees. We need to get on the ground again, to gape and tremble at God's greatness. The closer we stay to earth, the closer we are to heaven.

Are we too powerful to pray? Can we, like X-Men, swirl tornadoes, throw fire, and move bridges with our brains? Can we vanish on command or heal as quickly as we're hurt? Not so much! We need prayer like we need air. Human beings are made of mud and bones. We are a putty people who collapse when bullets pass our way.

Prayer is our power. It's our extension cord to the God who walks on water, withers fig trees, and tells rivers to do jumping jacks. Christ is the real superhero. He is the One who dueled with the Devil in the desert and changed the molecular structure of water into wine. He's the One who x-rayed hearts, hushed storms, and absorbed the evil of humanity. That's rather impressive! And if Christ had to pray, so must we. Jesus said, "I tell you the truth, anyone who has faith in me will do what I have been doing. He will do even greater things than these, because I am going to the Father" (John 14:12).

Before Jesus ascended into heaven, He promised to send down His Holy Spirit. It was a tag team of epic proportion. God exited and entered the ring on the same day. It's easy to ignore the role of the Holy Spirit and treat Him like the redheaded stepchild of the Trinity. But the Spirit has been given to us for a reason. He sends our prayers in the right direction. Like an antibiotic, He also defends us against the disease of worldliness. He is our teleprompter who feeds us words and our energy drink who pumps us up. But above all, the Holy Spirit points us to Jesus by putting flesh on our faith and bones on our Bibles.

Pig-Latin Prayers

When I was a kid I used to pray in pig Latin so the Devil couldn't decipher my words. It was a simple season of life, a season of Saturday morning cartoons and macaroni and cheese. I didn't know much back then, but I did assume that God could translate my six-year-old messages. After two years of pig Latin and a lot of weird looks in the cafeteria, I went back to praying in English. But every once in a while, just for fun, I'll begin the Lord's Prayer with "Our atherfay, who art in eavenhay . . ."

The discipline of prayer is at the very heart of the Christian experience. No other practice so sucks us into the volcanic presence of God. Of course, it's simple to pray in Cabbage Patch land when everything is smiles and giggles. But life has a way of rotting beneath our feet. Beds of roses become beds of nails, and problems, like a troop of pesky vultures, pick our lives to pieces. What then? How can we pray when the bottom of the bucket becomes the roof above our heads? How can we pray when our managers fire us or our friends betray us?

Christ loves crude prayers more than crafted ones.

In those miserable moments, we grunt our way to God. Flowery prayers drip like drool down our chins and we crawl to Christ, helpless and inarticulate. But Christians, like lilies, flourish in the shade. God tunes His ear to our frequency, and when no one else is listening, when all the world is deaf and absent, an antenna is aimed in our direction. Christ loves crude prayers more than crafted ones. And in our pain God touches us with His compassion.

What do we pray about? We often pray for ourselves: "Lord Jesus, Son of God, have mercy upon me, a sinner."[5] We also pray for exams, comforts, cars, and job promotions. But insular prayers grow boring after a while. It's tiring always being the subject of the sentence. God doesn't want to be our footnote; He seeks to be our title. It's time to elevate God with prayers that revolve around His ability and His beauty. God should rightfully occupy the center of our prayers. Only then can we pray with St. Patrick, "I arise today through a mighty strength, the invocation of the Trinity. Through belief in the threeness, through confession of the oneness of the Creator of creation."[6]

Christian Unity

Francis Schaeffer said that Jesus gives the world the right to judge whether we are Christians by our observable love for each other.[7] That means society can judge our relationship to God by our relationships to one another. A bold statement, indeed.

But it's a true one. God's canvas holds many colors—Baptist blue, Anglican red, Lutheran yellow, etc. Our commitment to love is the primer that supports our paint. Our commitment to stand together is the Velcro that binds us. Jesus said, "This is how everyone will recognize that you are my disciples—when they see the love you have for each other" (John 13:35 MESSAGE). There are many divisions in our churches today, but we are learning that our community on earth can reflect God's community in heaven. Our unity mimics His unity. Love is the tripod upholding the Trinity, and it is the heartbeat of our existence. When it comes to Christian unity, without apology we proclaim, "In essentials, unity; in nonessentials, liberty; in all things, charity."[8]

As our world gets smaller, our need for unity grows bigger. We do not live in isolation anymore. Technology has demolished our geographic barriers, and we are indeed existing in a global village. Even something as small as an iPod can revolutionize our sense of Christian togetherness. Just this morning I listened to a chanting community from France, a monastic Eucharist from Ireland, a prayer gathering from South Korea, and a healing service from Australia. And all before breakfast!

My generation, "the pilgrim generation," is naturally more ecumenical because we have a universal faith at our fingertips. We are the pilgrim generation because we are the traveling generation, the airport generation, moving more than any generation prior. International exposure has a way of putting things in perspective. We are discovering that other Christian traditions can transform our own. The universal church has something sacred to teach the local church. God is active in the lives of praying Christians across time and space. We are developing a kaleidoscopic Christianity that fights for unity in a world of great diversity.

It's become popular of late to reject the traditions of Christianity because the American church doesn't seem to be working. It's true that our prognosis doesn't look good. In fact, we are deathly ill. According to *unChristian*, by David Kinnaman and Gabe Lyons, America is a country of sedated saints. Our churches are packed with people, but spiritual laziness is at an all-time high. Spurgeon once said that just because a church is big doesn't mean it's healthy. It could just mean it's swollen.[9] Only the ice of the Holy Spirit can reduce our swelling. Only God can drain the fluids inflaming our faith.

The Asante people in Ghana, Africa, say, *yey boe m pie ey*, "let us kick prayer."[10] Their image of prayer involves a pulling back for the purpose of letting go. They punt their prayers to God, reaching back in order to move forward, pulling to push. They reach back into their week, into their month, gathering their mistakes and faults to shoot into the presence of God. That's how the Asante people score.

A Reaction Against the Past

Among many Christians today, there is a reaction against the past. We feel that we must "recast" Christianity because it's gone out of style. It's become popular to abandon our Christian roots, our historic practices, and start more or less from scratch.

But let's reject our condition, not our tradition.

The Bible instructs us to honor our fathers and mothers (Exodus 20:12). By completely ignoring the faith passed down to us, we disrespect those who sacrificed their lives so we can know God in a real and relevant way. We don't need to recast our faith; we need to recover it. Paul raises a good question: "What do you have that you did not receive? And if you did receive it, why do you boast as though you did not?" (1 Corinthians 4:7). God has accomplished great things throughout history. Simply leapfrogging back to the time of Jesus ignores what Jesus has been doing in the last two thousand years.

Our churches are dying, but we're not dead yet. We're in cardiac arrest. George Whitefield, the great revivalist who came to America, said, "The Christian world is in a deep sleep. Only a loud voice can awaken them out of it."[11] Only Christ can revive us. Revival always begins in the heart. Only then does it travel to the home, church, nation, continent, and world.

A Bigger View of a Holy and Glorified God

We need a bigger view of God—God who is Father, Son, and Spirit. Sometimes we ask God to show us His glory. We sing it and think it. Sometimes we even pray for it. But what if God answered our prayers? What if God truly showed us His glory? Would it blind or vaporize us? Would our faces shrivel like raisins from our skulls?

Probably. God told Moses, "No one can see me and live" (Exodus 33:20). In the Old Testament, God's glory resided in the temple. Once a year the chief priest alone would walk into the holy of holies with a rope tied around his foot. If he had sinned or was too careless in his approach, the glory of God killed him. Then the people, realizing he had not returned, would pull him out by the cord. They would not consider entering that most holy place. One time, a guy named Uzzah reached out to stabilize the ark of the covenant and the glory of God electrocuted him to death (1 Chronicles 13:7–10). If we truly saw the high-voltage glory of God, it would certainly be the end of us.

Glory shines, but it also bleeds.[12] The disciples were astonished when Jesus refused to demolish the Roman army and establish a martial stronghold. Their interpretation of Old Testament prophecies predicted a Jewish military hero. They wanted an Alexander the Great or a mighty Roman ruler. To their surprise Christ was a pauper, not a prince. He rode on donkeys, not in chariots. Yet Christ would be a conqueror of much more than mere first-century Roman occupation. Jesus had His eye on a bigger target—a darker enemy. And glory, it turned out, had leaky veins.

• • •

I still can't erase the memory of that fat drunk guy shaking his belly. Those three petals haunt me, jiggling in the crevices of my cranium. But they also remind me that God has minted Himself to humanity. His signature is stamped to our guts. God is beautiful despite our ugliness. He is muscular despite our fat rolls. And one day Christ, the Lily of the Valley, will parade through paradise, and we will throw beads before His throne.

Until then, you and I can parade the Trinity everywhere we go because we are made in God's image. His breath is on our lips. His words are in our hands. And that is why Christians can stand together and serve together. As soccer unites the world, prayer unites God's people. We can play together and pray together because one day we will praise together—catching crowns on streets of gold.

"The fastest way to a man's heart
is through Jack Bauer's gun."

—the musings of a die-hard fan of Fox-TV's 24

2 Jesus Ninja

• • •

God's Power \ˈpou(-ə)r\

There's something magical about the city of Rome. Maybe it's the weathered cobblestone streets laced with mopeds and pizzerias. Or it could be the fountains, regurgitating water from naked gods and swimming things. Perhaps it's the grassy marble, or the way the sun licks the architecture, leaving an orange mist that settles on the city.

Eighteen hundred years ago, Rome was hot stuff. Their military was envied and their government, exemplary. They even perfected indoor plumbing. Not too bad considering the first indoor American toilet appeared in 1829.[1] As I stood near the Roman Forum, sandwiched between modern tourists and ancient history, I caught a glimpse of my shadow. I'm no gladiator, but with the sun to my back it stretched for thirty feet or more. I moved, it moved. I jumped, it jumped. I felt more powerful than Caesar, spreading my arms to form a wingspan the length of a Hummer. Of course when the sun disappeared, I returned to a 5 foot 8 inch American white boy making a fool of himself in public.

A Dangerous Divinity

The psalmist wrote, "Our Lord is great, with limitless strength" (Psalm 147:5 MESSAGE). In other words, God's shadow is light-years long. He stretches His hammock from the Statue of Liberty to the Coliseum in Rome.

His power is telescopic. But it's also microscopic. God swirls both the planet and the proton. He surfs through arteries and confronts viruses face-to-face. Christians do not worship a gambling God—a God who risks. There are no rogue molecules in this world. Every atom awaits His orders, and we know what happens when one of those splits.

Albert Einstein admitted, "I am convinced that [God] does not play dice."[2] God is so powerful that He's not even bound by the laws He created. He's a dangerous divinity. Gravity levitates before Him. Water solidifies beneath Him. He flips galaxies like omelets against the sizzling blackness. It's easy to play theological limbo and see how low our view of God can go. Sometimes we even treat Him like He needs a shot of espresso to get up in the morning.

But there is something satisfying about recovering a sense of the power of God. We are discovering the Christ who wields the sword and the scalpel. Nothing is too big or little for His skills. When it comes to evil, humans are not white belts. But like a ninja, Jesus steals from us what we cannot surrender.[3] Sin bows before Christ, its sensei. And with David we shout, "Exalted be the God of my salvation . . . He delivers me from my enemies" (Psalm 18:46 NASB). And later, "If you're kicked in the gut, he'll help you catch your breath" (Psalm 34:18 MESSAGE).

Sometimes we want a housebroken God, a domesticated Deity. We want a jack-in-the-box Jesus who appears at our command.

But God is wilder than that, and hairier, too. He's not the clean-shaven gentleman we pretend He is. We want an Easter bunny, but God's a tyrannosaurus rex—a growling King who protects His cubs from the enemy, who "prowls around like a roaring lion looking for someone to devour" (1 Peter 5:8).

But He's also an anteater—the smallest threat is a big deal to Him. Christians can trust a God like that. The Omnipotent isn't impotent. God's strength is stronger than our weaknesses. But what if the tables were turned? What if God were fickle instead of faithful? What if He had changed His mind at the last minute and sent a phalanx of Jackie Chan angels to save Christ from the Roman soldiers, to hack through their weapons and pull the Son of God from the tree of death? That's what the Greek gods would have done. Zeus, Athena, and Hermes acted on impulses rather than covenants.

But God is different. "I will surely save you," He told the nation of Israel (Jeremiah 30:10). No matter how many times we drop the ball, God still controls the game. His plans are etched in marble, not pencil. His love is carved in stone, not in Styrofoam. Humans are not tall creatures, but we do worship a tall God. A venti God, if we're ordering at Starbucks. Most of us can't even bench-press our own weight, much less hoist ourselves to Christ. But God lowers Himself to us. He secures us inside His vault and throws away the key.

Obedience

Not a Gigabyte

According to Karl Barth, one of the greatest theologians of the twentieth century, "Knowledge of God is obedience to God."[4] Only when we understand the sovereignty of God—*His* freedom and *His* ability—can we understand ours. Christians are not robots, lacking the power to make real choices. We're made of guts, not gigabytes.

Yet in God's mysterious mainframe, our decisions run in

harmony with His program. God's *yin* does not negate our *yang*. It's impossible to see how it all works together on earth. When we're playing on the field, with our helmets on, we can barely see one another, much less the big picture. But God sits in the control booth. His perspective is higher than ours; His view is superior. Spurgeon was once asked how He reconciles God's sovereignty and human freedom. He responded, "I never reconcile friends."[5] The choices we make in life are determined by our desires. Our desires are determined by our natures. If our natures are sinful (Romans 3), we will naturally choose what is wrong.

But here's the mystery: God has given us new natures. Our upgrade comes with new hardware. God saws through our skulls and replaces worldly minds with minds of Christ. We have new desires, and therefore we make unnatural choices. Choices like living in opposition to the presuppositions of society. Choices like abandoning the nonessentials of life to live and work among the poor. These are radical choices, but we are free to make them. And the world asks, "So where's the tax shelter?"

Obedience must become a discipline for us because it is unnatural. Our very nation was born in disobedience. When King George III of Britain raised the taxes on American colonies, we turned the Boston Harbor into a giant teacup and eventually won our independence. We Americans pride ourselves on our reaction against authority. Being raised in a postmodern, western environment, I confess that I am the first to be suspicious of institutionalism. Whether it's a white-collar multibillion-dollar business, a government agency, or just a company running a winsome infomercial, I'm often skeptical of organizations.

Obedience to God takes many practical forms. It can be as routine as getting up thirty minutes before dawn to soak in the Scripture. Or it can be as spontaneous as pulling off to the side of the road to change someone's tire. God loves organic obedience just as much as organized obedience. The key is self-abandonment. John the Baptist declared, "Jesus must become more important, while I become less important" (John 3:30 CEV). But we don't like that. We like to be at the center of the stage, the object of applause. The crowd must clap for us, not Christ. But when we practice the discipline of obedience, we discover that there's more to God's musical than our own short solos. There's more to His symphony than our brief melodies. And by dethroning ourselves, we applaud the God who gets the encore.

Humans spend lots of energy *doing*. We even define our friends by what they do instead of who they are. "Oh, he's a lawyer, or a musician, or an engineer." Production is the marrow of our mentalities. But humans also need to spend time *being*. The Christian faith is not just outward. It's also inward. We must care enough for others to care for ourselves. Every flight attendant knows that you have to place the oxygen mask on yourself first, then your child. Why? Because if you're unconscious, your child will be also.

There are two kinds of people in this world: those who live outside-in and those who live inside-out. The outside-in folks allow the world to saturate their thinking. They are sponges, absorbing the agendas of this world without a filter. Like the Roman Empire, they are destroyed from within. In contrast, those who live inside-out change the world with what's inside them. They splurge in truth and spill it to everyone around. It's the difference between a black hole and a burning star. It's more beautiful to explode in light than implode in darkness. And we all know that there are enough black holes in this world already.

The Roman Empire operated on a strict discipline of obedience. They understood that a successful military depended on a chain of command. Insubordination was punishable by death.[6] When the apostle Paul wrote his letter to the Christians living in Rome, he applauded them for many things, but primarily for their obedience: "Everyone has heard about your obedience, so I am full of joy over you" (Romans 16:19).

Paul recognized the importance of this discipline. After years of beatings and jailings, he did not abandon the mission to spread the gospel throughout the world. For Paul, obedience to Christ meant outreach to others—we go out because God came down. We'll never fully unravel the mystery of God's sovereignty and human freedom, but this we know: the master plan of salvation involves human participation. God's blueprints include our sketchings.

Sharing the Story

Back in high school, I was a DC Talk fanatic. I bought all their CDs, knew all their lyrics, and hung their poster above my bed. But one day, not long after I received my driver's license, I was speeding through Birmingham with my windows down blaring "Jesus Is Still Alright with Me." I was really getting into it—slapping my steering wheel, bobbing my head to the beat.

Then my gas light came on. I turned into a Shell station and pulled up beside a green, decked-out Cadillac. Its subwoofer rattled my rear-view mirror and I looked over at the four guys dancing in their seats. Suddenly, their music stopped and they turned to look at me. Without hesitation, I scrambled to mute my song so they couldn't hear my Christian music. But it was too late. A stroke of embarrassment rushed down my spine as smiles emerged on their faces. I desperately needed gas, but I drove away. To this day, I can still feel that surge of shame creep up and down my body, and Paul's words disembowel me: "I am not ashamed of the gospel, because it is the power of God for the salvation of everyone who believes" (Romans 1:16).

Evangelism is not a popular word in our world. It's not like *tolerant* or *open-minded* or *progressive*. Evangelism rubs us the wrong way because we live in an age that resists absolute truth. What's true for me doesn't have to be true for you. But biblical evangelism, the kind Paul did, says that there is one source of truth. Everything else is false. So when Jesus said, "I am the way and the truth and the life. No one comes to the Father except through me" (John 14:6), that puts us in a difficult position. It means we have to put our "don't step on my toes and I won't step on yours" mentality in the trunk and speak the truth in love, even when it's not trendy. It means we don't have to be ashamed of the gospel, even when it comes through a car speaker system at full volume. To be a Christian is to swim upstream and remind people of the waterfall on the horizon.

In Roman times, mirrors were often small and made of bronze. Instead of modern, pristine mirrors, ancient mirrors produced a darker reflection.[7] This explains Paul's comment, "Now we see but a poor reflection as in a mirror" (1 Corinthians 13:12). On this side of eternity, we don't have all the answers. We swim in the sea of mystery. Yet it's so much more beautiful to be a person of faith than doubt. To be a person who believes in something beyond yourself. Who would you rather read on a rainy Sunday afternoon—Friedrich Nietzsche who claimed that God is dead, or C. S. Lewis who believed that God is life?

God's story is more than just a myth. It's more than just a human endeavor to cope with a difficult universe. Christ really lives, He really changes lives, and He really is coming back again. In His own words, "So you also must be ready, because the Son of Man will come at an hour when you do not expect him" (Matthew 24:44).

There are many views on the second coming of Christ, but one thing is clear: Our lives are like a mist that appears for a little while and then vanishes (James 4:14). Like egg rolls at a sumo wrestling convention, you and I don't last very long. Rome wasn't built in a day, but it was practically destroyed in one. And because our time is restricted, because our duration is limited, we need a steroid kind of hope. We need a hope that motivates the here and now. A Christian without hope is a snowboarder without snow—it makes for a very bumpy ride.

We keep on looking. We keep on waiting. We spread the love and hope of God without apology or embarrassment. Life is too short for shame. Eternity is too long for laziness. In his book *Your God Is Too Small*, J. B. Phillips writes, "The trouble with many people today is that they have not found a God big enough for modern needs."[8] But we're not done looking. Instead, we're just beginning. We are taking another look at Jesus—a fresher look. A look that doesn't overlook His command to "go into the world. Go everywhere and announce the Message of God's good news to one and all" (Mark 16:15 MESSAGE). A kudzu Christianity grows before us—a life that spreads from person to person, from city to city, until the whole country, the whole generation, the whole world is green with spiritual health.

So turn up your music. Hit the repeat button on your faith. God's story is not predictable, but it's certain. And unlike the Roman Empire, God's kingdom lasts forever. Jesus is coming back again. We don't know when or where or how, but one thing's for sure: Objects in mirror are closer than they appear.

"Anybody hear that?"

—*Dr. Ian Malcolm in* Jurassic Park

3

Sunsets and Dinosaurs

• • •

God's Creativity \ˈkrē-ā-ˈti-vi-tē\

Once upon a time, everything was silent. There were no jazz clubs, infomercials, or thunderstorms. There were no barking dogs or honking horns. It was untamed tranquility.

And then God spoke. Perhaps a word, then a sentence. From the same throat came three chords—Father, Son, and Spirit—a holy harmonic. Suddenly, stars burst into being and planets got their spins on. Elephants and oceans were formed, along with beetles, eagles, and raspberries. It was a flawless painting, a perfect painting, a sunset that took six days to dry. And there were colors that made rainbows look like ashtrays.

Soon God formed man from dust and then breathed into his nostrils the breath of life (Genesis 2:7). Can you hear it? It's the noise that comes from our mouths when we fog up our glasses. Suddenly the dead became the living.

Recently, I found myself looking through the lenses of a telescope. It wasn't the Hubble, but I could see craters on the moon. The moon's waxing grin was dented with dimples, and it was smiling at me. It was smirking at the little human who thought he was big enough to lose his temper at the McDonald's employee who gave him a Happy Meal instead of a Big Mac. It was snickering at the man who was big enough to walk right past the homeless guy on 5th Avenue as he begged for anything more than a nickel.

As I looked up into the blackness, Job's words came to mind: "Why, even the moon has its flaws, even the stars aren't perfect in God's eyes, so how much less, plain men and women—slugs and maggots by comparison" (Job 25:5–6 MESSAGE). The strangest feeling came over me. I was the one on display, not the moon. And my telescope was His microscope.

The common housefly is more complicated than our most sophisticated fighter plane.

Charles Spurgeon said, "We speak of power, but the heavens laugh us to scorn."[1] Of course they do. Our planet is the comedy club for the solar system. The heavens declare the glory of God, but we declare our own glory. We make intricate computers but still can't wrap our minds around the wiring of the human brain. We build elaborate skyscrapers but still can't control the earthquakes that tremble beneath them. We even launch airplanes that fly from Atlanta to London in seven hours. But if the weather is bad, if the skies are too dangerous, even our biggest jets are grounded. All the while there is God, holding the layout for every design He ever created.

Biomimetics is the study of nature for the purpose of technological design. For example, scientists study the molecular structure of shark skin to create Speedos with reduced drag. Or they observe nanohairs on gecko feet to invent wall-climbing equipment. Even whale flippers are used as templates for turbine blades. Did you know that the common housefly is more complicated than our most sophisticated fighter plane? Its wings beat a hundred and fifty times per second and it takes 90 degree turns at 50 milliseconds. That torque would tear an F-16 in two.[2] Ronald Fearing, professor of electrical engineering at the University of California, Berkeley, noted, "The fly's wing is driven by twenty muscles, some of which only fire every fifth wing beat, and all you can do is wonder, 'What on earth just happened there?' Some things are just too mysterious and complicated to be able to replicate."[3]

In other words, God's creative juices never dry out. The grapes of His genius never turn to raisins. "By taking a long and thoughtful look at what God has created, people have always been able to see . . . the mystery of His divine being" (Romans 1:20), wrote the apostle Paul. Job saw God's creation when he looked at the behemoth, a grass-eating beast who had bones of bronze and trees for tails (Job 40). And the leviathan, a fire-breathing sea dragon with jagged teeth and multiple heads (Job 41, Psalm 74:14). But even the stubborn triceratops bows its three-horned head in God's presence. Velociraptors curtsey before Him. Even King Kong quits his monkey business when God shows his teeth.

A Re-Created Life

God creates us, but He also re-creates us. Every seven years the human body regenerates itself. Human cells are constantly being recycled. We get new skeletons, kidneys, ankles, and ears. We get new tongues, hearts, toenails, and clavicles. In other words, the bodies we wear today are not the bodies we put on seven years ago. Even more spectacular is the fact that our atoms are not our own. According to science author Bill Bryson, atoms are extremely durable: "When we die our atoms will disassemble and move off to find new uses elsewhere—as part of a leaf or other human being."[4] So it's certainly possible, and according to Bryson even plausible, that the atoms of Elvis or Beethoven, even Hitler or Stalin, are circulating in or near us. Even on a molecular level, Solomon was right: "There is nothing new under the sun" (Ecclesiastes 1:9).

Because the body of Jesus never decayed, God enters His people another way—a better way. John the apostle wrote, "As many as receive him become the sons of God" (John 1:12; my paraphrase). It doesn't take seven years for that regeneration to happen. God instantly guts us. We are immediately renovated. And like the wind that "blows wherever it pleases" (John 3:8), the Holy Spirit gusts Himself on those He loves.

When God enters us, we not only become holy, we become "greater poets, greater artists, and greater lovers of God and of His universe."[5] Why? Because God is artistically oriented and He seeks to share His inclination with His re-made creatures. But art is rarely considered a spiritual discipline. It's not like fasting, praying, or meditating. It's not like studying, retreating, or labyrinth walking. It's not even clearly prescribed in the Scriptures. But by surrendering to God the creativity that He has given to us, we deepen our spiritual awareness. By sketching a sunset or pointing at planets, we adore the God who paints the sky and hangs the heavens.

In the Old Testament, God was very concerned about the decoration of His tent. He told Moses, "See what I've done; I've personally chosen Bezalel. . . . I've filled him with the Spirit of God, giving him skill and know-how and expertise in every kind of craft to create designs and work in gold, silver, and bronze; to cut and set gemstones, to carve wood—he's an all-around craftsman" (Exodus 31:2–5 MESSAGE). When it came to tent and temple artwork, God had a no slackers policy.

But we don't have to paint like Picasso to please God. Sometimes a walk in the woods is enough. Jonathan Edwards, the greatest American theologian, spent hundreds of hours in the Connecticut forests, sketching spiders, insects, and trees. He noted, "Every new discovery must necessarily raise in us a fresh sense of the greatness, wisdom, and power of God."[6] John Calvin said, "There is not one blade of grass, there is no color in this world that is not intended to make us rejoice."[7] For Edwards and Calvin, studying nature's design gave them better glimpses of nature's Designer.

A Textured Life

As we move from a physical world to a digital one—from fine art to graphic design—an interesting development is underway. We are beginning to crave the textured life. In a day when most of our communication occurs online and iPhoto replaces tangible albums, we are beginning to hunger for the grainy life, the touchable life. We need the nitty-gritty. Face-to-face communities are becoming crucial again, along with eye-to-eye interaction. Technology will continue to shape the future, but it's also shaping us. It can numb and distance us from what our souls were created to experience—walking with God in the cool of the day (Genesis 3:8). I'm not talking about taking an interactive virtual walking tour, but rather, a breezy, creek wading, muscle stretching jaunt with Jesus.

The discipline of art connects us to the Artist. But it's not limited to pigments. Art can also be applied to paragraphs. Words are magical creatures. Robert Browning said, "God is the perfect poet."[8] The book of Psalms, for instance, is one giant collection of poetry. In English, rhyme is the prime driver of our poetry. But in Hebrew, poets used repetition, acrostics, and rhythm to express artistic beauty. The Psalms were meant to be sung, not said. David, the "man after God's own heart" (1 Samuel 13:14), played the harp and often lost himself in divine melody. In English the Psalms glow, but in Hebrew—they're a laser light show. Yet, no matter what our language or poetic skill, every one of us can offer art to God. Don't laugh, but here's my stab at it:

If

If God were a tree I would climb Him.
        Hanging from jagged branches
until twigs like fingers itched me to embrace
        His knotted holiness.

If God were a shirt I would wear Him.
        Shedding soiled clothes
for silk that clings to every inch of me,
        my soul, so wet and warm.

If God were a steak I would eat Him.
        Purging past failures to
sheath my teeth in veins
        that knew the nails.

Since God was a man I can love Him.
        Breathing His waves like air
until grace as bubbles
        brings me to the surface of enchantment.

Rhythm and Worship

Carl Sagan once said, "If you want to make an apple pie from scratch, you must first create the universe."[9] His point is well taken. Nothing in our lives is truly original. Everything we offer to God has been offered before—every feeling, every sacrifice, every burden. Yet the beauty of worship is that we are the ones offering it. For us, it is a first-time event, a brand-new present. And for this very reason, worship can be an act of art.

From the time of Noah, humans have been building altars to God. Some were for sacrifice, others for memory. When the Israelites crossed into the Promised Land, they built stone altars to remember God's miracles. After crossing the Jordan, God instructed one man from each of the twelve tribes to take a stone with him. These stones would remind the next generation of God's deliverance (Joshua 4).

Over the years, the landscape of Israel became a three-dimensional diary, dotted with rocks and altars that pointed to God's goodness. God told them to write down His teaching on these stones: "Incise them sharply," He commanded (Deuteronomy 27:8). When pilgrims traveled to Jerusalem every year for the holy festivals, they encountered these stones—these tactile memories—and were visually stimulated to worship. Poems like Psalm 23 were sung to comfort weary travelers who often passed through the valley of the shadow of death. For them, these rocks were tangible reminders of grace anchored in the past.

But we also look to the future. What does twenty-first-century worship look like? Cyber churches. No longer must we be physically present to hear a sermon, sing a song, or even take communion. All you have to do is create an animated character and walk into an artificial sanctuary.[10]

Now, perhaps God can be worshiped in this way, but as we progress into the future I'm sensing a genuine attraction to the past—to authentic, hands-on worship. Jesus didn't come to earth as a pixel; He came as a person. He didn't just send us a text message; He knocked on our doors. Because we are taking another look at Christ's physical descent, we are beginning to crave shoulder-to-shoulder and face-to-face community again.

Not long ago, my dream of visiting the Holy Land became a reality. For years I sought that place—to travel through Galilee to see the stones that God sat and spat upon. And I'll never forget walking down Jerusalem's Via Dolorosa, "the way of suffering," the traditional route Jesus took with His cross. I had seen pictures of it in books and magazines, but to actually stand there, to feel it beneath my feet, was altogether sacred.

Undistracted by Arabs selling trinkets made in China, I followed the footsteps of Jesus. Holding a miniature cross, I tried to imagine Christ's burden. Each step brought me closer to the traditional place where Jesus was crucified—the Church of the Holy Sepulcher, a site shared by various Christian traditions including Greeks, Latins, Egyptians, Syrians, and Ethiopians. As I knelt to the floor, surrounded by a mosaic of worshiping Christ-followers, I came to the conclusion that every Christian walks the grueling path of grief. Not just me, or my friends, or my tradition. The road of suffering belongs to *all* of God's people. Like Simon from Cyrene, every one of us has the privilege of temporarily carrying Christ's burden (Mark 15:21). Despite our worship styles, Christians share the same path. So why should we walk divided on earth when we will live united in heaven? True worship is a life of rhythm. It's a life of seasons, some sunny, some stormy.

Walking down Jerusalem's Via Dolorosa . . . to feel it beneath my feet, was altogether sacred.

The Celts knew this. There's an island called Skellig Michael off the Irish coast where the monks kept track of the church calendar not by the sun or moon, but by the migration of the birds. Every year thousands of puffins would flock to these rocks (they still do), and to live there among them was to experience a cyclical rhythm of nature that emphasized the *now*. The psalmist asked God to "teach us to number our days" (Psalm 90:12 NASB). As busy as we are, we tend to live in the tomorrow. Our calendars stretch months in advance, and it becomes easy to ignore the present moment. But there is a benefit of finding a rhythm of life that lets us live each day to the fullest. Between the cosmic calendar and the Christian calendar a wondrous dance takes place,[11] and when we discover it, we can harmonized our lives with God's created cadence.

As worship gains traction among us twentysomething Christians, we are being drawn to older, more reverent forms of worship—a sacred encounter with Christ. Some churches appeal to the culture by compromising the core values of Christianity. But in the process of becoming relevant, they've become completely and utterly irrelevant. Their identities have dissolved.

But the American church can put her name tag on again. We can once more take seriously the traditional elements of our faith—elements like reading the Scriptures, enjoying the Lord's Supper, preaching a God-centered sermon, praying, and worshiping Christ in Spirit and in truth. We can go back to the basics, back to the incarnational way of life—the sounds and smells, tastes and touch, of Christianity. Like Smeagol's fish in J. R. R. Tolkien's *Lord of the Rings*, we want our faith as raw as possible.

• • •

According to astrophysicists, 1 percent of the universe is composed of stars, and up to 99 percent is dark matter[12]—a measurable form of matter that does not reflect electromagnetic radiation. In other words, most everything that exists is invisible. I'm no scientist (just ask my high school chemistry teacher), but here we go: Everything we know is made of atomic particles—this book, your hand, even the light that allows you to read these words. Inside these atoms are nuclei composed of protons and neutrons. Protons and neutrons are made up of tiny particles called quarks. Quarks are held together by gluons that we can't see, but know must exist. But what are gluons? It's at this point that scientists scratch their heads.

Yet Christians might have a clue. According to the apostle Paul, "He [Christ] is the image of the invisible God, the firstborn over all creation. For by him all things were created: things in heaven and on earth, visible and *invisible,* whether thrones or powers or rulers or authorities; all things were created by him and for him. He is before all things, and *in him all things hold together*" (Colossians 1:15–17, italics mine). Isn't God the glue that holds His creation together? Can't the Creator also be the Sustainer? God asked Jeremiah, "Am I not present everywhere, whether seen or unseen?" (Jeremiah 23:24).

God's not done creating. He's actually just beginning. Up until now, He's been painting the background. But a day is coming when the foreground will fall into place. John wrote, "Then I saw a new heaven and a new earth, for the first heaven and the first earth had passed away, and there was no longer any sea. I saw the Holy City, the new Jerusalem, coming down out of heaven from God" (Revelation 21:1–2). Until that city is set in stone, Christians travel side by side through this world. We continue scratching our stories into rock, reminding those behind us of God's generosity. Most of all, we can live each day like the last chapter of our lives will be our very first.

"What can you say about a society that says that God is dead and Elvis is alive?"

—Irv Kupcinet

4

Showing Some Skin

• • •

God's Vulnerability \vəl-n(ə)r-ə-ˈbil-i-tē\

Let's get right down to business. Jesus took off His clothes. From the beginning of time, He planned to do it—trading heavenly silk for soiled humanity. And in obedience to His Father, He came to earth as a man. "What can be stranger than God in a manger?" asks one song lyric.[1]

What a thought! That God would feel the fever of infection and the throb of a headache. The apostle Paul wrote, "When the time came, he set aside the privileges of deity and took on the status of a slave" (Philippians 2:7 MESSAGE). And God stripped Himself that we might be clothed.

The Scriptures say, "The Word became flesh and made his dwelling among us" (John 1:14). It's so easy to read this passage at warp speed and forget the severity of this vulgarity. Jesus knew pain firsthand. He was not an airbrushed model who never knew a wart or wrinkle. No, God became real blood and real bone. "The infinite has become an infant."[2]

Nothing in art or music can match this mystery. Mozart can't play it. Michelangelo can't paint it. Even the great Leonardo da Vinci in his *Last Supper* waited until the very end to paint the portrait of Jesus. After much frustration he quickly sketched His face and said, "There's no use. I can't paint Him." It's impossible to trace Christ's silhouette.

How can Jesus be fully God and fully man? The early church wrestled with this question. Some believed that God could never become a man because matter was evil. Gnostic teacher Marcion believed Jesus was a just a ghost and couldn't appear in the flesh.

America doesn't know what to do with the identity of Jesus.

In AD 325, Roman Emperor Constantine wanted to settle the dispute over Jesus once and for all, and he held a debate at Nicea (modern-day Turkey). In one corner of the ring you have Athanasius, who correctly argued that Jesus was 100 percent God and 100 percent man. On the other side was Arius, who taught that Jesus was just one of God's creations and therefore less than God. By the end of the fight, Arius got the smack down because his teachings weren't consistent with biblical truth, and everyone knew it.

Why does this matter to us, seventeen hundred years later? Because these beliefs are being regurgitated and propagated in our culture. Just ask Oprah, possibly the most influential person on television, who said that if Jesus had claimed exclusive divinity, He would be "the biggest egotist that ever lived."[3] Look at the popularity of *The Da Vinci Code*, in which Dan Brown wrote, "The Church needed to convince the world that the mortal prophet Jesus was a divine being."[4] Generally, America doesn't know what to do with the identity of Jesus. Two out of five American adults (42 percent) believe that when Jesus was on earth, He sinned.[5]

Before the birth of Christ, the Jews believed that the Messiah would be a military hero with guns blazing and grenades flying. They wanted God to deliver them from Roman bondage, but to their surprise God did just the opposite. He came down, not in a pin-striped suit, but in coarse clothing—a semi-naked man from Nazareth who was mocked, ridiculed, and spit on. How odd of God! But by becoming an ordinary guy with ordinary problems, Jesus could pray to His Father, "You've concealed your ways from sophisticates and know-it-alls, but spelled them out clearly to ordinary people" (Matthew 11:26 MESSAGE).

Jesus understands what it's like to be in our skin. He walked a mile not only in our shoes, but also in our feet. Our veins were His veins. Our blood was His blood. He knew the agony, numbness, and intensity of being human. He felt the rush of adrenaline and the sneeze of a cold. He suffered from fears and doubts, maybe ingrown toenails and acid indigestion. No other god took so radical a jump as Jesus. Buddha didn't. Brahma, Vishnu, and Apollo didn't. The *incarnation* (literally "into flesh") is unique to Christianity because the kamikaze Christ plunged into death that we might have life. That's why Christ sees through our clothes, through our facades, even to the core of us. Because Jesus was man, God identifies with us. Because Jesus was divine, we identify with God.

Smelly Flesh

During the Dark Ages, Christians living in England, Ireland, and Scotland copied Bibles by hand onto animal skin. Since the printing press hadn't been invented, this was a painstaking process. A single page often took a whole year to complete. The Book of Kells, for instance, took 185 calfskins to create. After killing the animal, the skin would be soaked in lime and water for several weeks. The scribes would scrape off the hair, then stretch, dry, and cut it. For the Celts, each page was a tangible reminder that the Word really became hot, smelly, hairy skin.

Let's be honest: We've got Bibles coming out of our ears—KJV, NKJV, NAS, NRSV, NIV—black-leathered, tan-sueded, hard-and soft-covered, alligator-bound, etc. We have specialized Bibles for every occasion and audience: audio Bibles, army Bibles, archeology Bibles, teenage Bibles, leadership Bibles, women's devotional Bibles, and the list goes on and on. The crisp, thin pages of our Scriptures are easily printed and often sit on our shelves, untouched and unread.

But for the Celts, the Scriptures were rare and special. Each copy was difficult to come by. They were carefully crafted and dressed with artwork. It's the difference between a mass manufactured Honda CR-V (no offense; I own one) and a hand-built, custom-designed 599 GTB Fiorano Ferrari. In other words, *huge* difference. To flip through the pages of the Book of Kells with its sophisticated interlacing and geometric color rhythms was to remember a holy moment, a humbling moment, when God tattooed Himself to humanity by mingling the sacred with the secular.

The Celts were fleshy people. Check out this prayer for protection, found on the Breastplate of Laidcenn:

> O God, defend me everywhere, deliver all my mortal limbs,
> so the demons shall not hurl their darts into my side.
>
> Be a breastplate for my innards, forehead, eyes, and tri-form brain,
> Snout, lip, face, nipples, temple, tongue, and uvula.
>
> Protect my larynx and epiglottis, fists, palms, fingers with their nails.
> Calves, femurs, ankles, ribs, back and blood.

Protect my three cornered liver and groin, pouch, kidneys,
intestines with its fold.
Protect my bladder, fat, veins, spleen and bile with its eruption.

Protect my hair and all the remaining members
which I have perhaps omitted.
So that by leaving the flesh I may escape the depths
and fly to the heights.
And by the mercy of God be born anew in his kingdom.[6]

Prayers like these emerged out of a deep appreciation for God's love for His creatures. It wasn't enough for God to create a femur; He had to stand on one. It wasn't enough for God to create a finger; He had to point with one. And by becoming a man with real bumps and bruises, God intensified His relationship with us. He went from the third person to the first and saw life through our retinas. God cares about the small things—tongues, snouts, and bladders—and a no-holds-barred approach to faith allows us to express our gratitude to the God who showed some skin in the person of Jesus Christ.

Journaling

Blogging for the Soul

Journaling is an inward practice that reminds us of an upward reality—that God glued Himself to our planet. By inscribing our thoughts and prayers on paper, we appreciate Christ's condescension. Journaling is a celebration of the incarnation.

Humans are forgetful creatures. Try going a month without a calendar and see what happens (really bad things, as I've learned). So if our memories can't sustain our professional lives, why do we trust them with our spiritual lives? Journaling is a way of remembering what God has done in the past. It helps us spiritually assess ourselves and gives clarity to our lives by recording our progress and regress.

What's the best way to begin? For starters, get a notebook you'd be proud to write in. You don't have to skin a cow, but the pages should be durable enough to withstand the ups and downs of a spiritual journey. People journal at different times. Some journal on pilgrimages and spiritual retreats to focus on God without the distraction of routine. Others journal on weekends to debrief from the stresses of work.

As a general rule, journaling is most successful when done daily. In my life, it doesn't always happen that way. I guess that's why they call it a discipline. But there is something healthy about reading a Bible verse in the morning, absorbing its truth throughout the day, and then journaling its implications at night. By doing so, life becomes less of a rush and more of a rhythm. We inhale God's Word, process its power, and exhale its application. The result is beautiful—God-moments in every moment.

Journals are blogs for the soul . . . records of our hopes, prayers, fears, meditations, and insights.

Journals are blogs for the soul. They're chronological records of our hopes, songs, prayers, fears, regrets, meditations, and insights. They are inky memories awaiting constant review. Because the Christian path is seldom smooth, journaling reminds us that struggles don't last forever. Every pilgrim needs a mile marker, and journals encourage us to continue on the journey.

This discipline not only sharpens our spiritual lives, but it also encourages others in theirs. Granted, sharing a journal is like opening an artery onto a piece of paper. It's painful, and often bloody. But history is scattered with those who weren't afraid to squirt some emotion. From the *Confessions* of Saint Augustine to the *Journals of Jim Elliot*, the most inspirational writings are coated with triumphs and tragedies.

Monks and Martyrs

Journaling is a private discipline that reflects the incarnation, but serving others *is* the incarnation for those around us. Look at the last words of Jesus: "What you'll get is the Holy Spirit. And when the Holy Spirit comes on you, you will be able to be my witnesses in Jerusalem, all over Judea and Samaria, even to the ends of the world" (Acts 1:7–8 MESSAGE). We aren't just God's torso, we're His limbs. "Real religion, the kind that passes muster before God the Father, is this: Reach out to the homeless" (James 1:27 MESSAGE).

By getting in sync with God's work in our lives, our eyes are opened to those around us. A sign outside a cathedral in Philadelphia reads, "How can you worship a homeless Man on Sunday morning and ignore one on Monday?" While the "social gospel" often becomes all social and no gospel,[7] every one of us is responsible to Christ for those around us. God forgive us for being catatonic Christians standing still in a world of falling people.

A rugged, earthy form of Christianity is spreading throughout our culture—a new kind of monasticism. Taking seriously God's command to feed the hungry and clothe the naked, small communities are springing up from Oregon to New York. Scot Bessenecker, director of global projects for InterVarsity Christian Fellowship, finds "an emerging movement of youth taking up residence in slum communities in the same spirit that I find in the start of the Franciscans and the early Celtic orders."[8]

Shane Claiborne, author of *The Irresistible Revolution,* writes, "The kingdom that Jesus speaks so much about is not just something we hope for after we die but is something we are to incarnate now."[9] Like Celtic monks who shared their possessions and lived frugally in Ireland, American monks are recovering a simple life, a serving life, a life radically devoted to hands-on ministry.

Christianity is not only a call to live, it's also a call to suffer. Jesus told His disciples, "If they persecuted me, they will persecute you also" (John 15:20). Since America was founded on principles of religious liberty, it's hard for us to understand the persecution that Christians around the world face from their governments. Richard Wurmbrand, a Romanian pastor, spent fourteen years being tortured in communist prisons. His journals have opened our eyes to the struggles of Christians around the world. "The gospel," he writes, "is the privilege of becoming a member of the body of Christ, of suffering, of dying in pain with Him, and also of being resurrected with Him in glory."[10]

For guys like me who've never spent a single night in jail, it's difficult to imagine yearlong imprisonments and endless hours of torture—being drowned, resuscitated, and then starved. Hunger is foreign to me. I live in a culture that's overfed and overweight. How can we identify with those whose bellies are bloated with hunger when ours are so swollen with food? How can manicured fingers have anything in common with tortured toes?

Our spiritual health is hardly better. We have a fat-roll faith, clogged by the consumption of worldliness. Mother Teresa, who spent her life feeding hungry people in India, was shocked at the physical and spiritual condition of America. It blew her mind that we spend so much money taking calories *out* of the food we eat. Against the backdrop of our great wealth she commented, "You in the West have the spiritually poorest of the poor."[11]

We have much to learn from those who are suffering on the front lines of faith. They need God in a way we will never know. *They* are the ones in the spotlight, not us. They are the ones on stage, shining so brightly against the darkness. We are simply their supporting cast—their backstage crew—and it's time we stop stealing the show. "In my prison cell," Wurmbrand wrote, "Jesus' presence was immediate."[12] Our problem is that we don't crave the nearness of Christ. We keep Him at a distance, far from the comforts He might tell us to abandon. We want a controlled Christianity, a straightjacketed Savior, a safe faith. And our worship services are so soporific that if God woke up, we'd be the last to know.

But God's alarm clock has just gone off. The post-boomer generation is getting out of bed. We're tired of worshiping a God who yawns at our faith. We're beginning to stand up to the challenges that come from cultivating a living, breathing, risking faith.

We want a controlled Christianity, a straightjacketed Savior, a safe faith.

We don't have to be monks or martyrs to experience Christ's presence. But we do need a healthy prayer life. Thanks to the satellite-mapping program Google Earth, Christians can take virtual prayer walks through closed countries. We can visually fly over North Korea and pray for villages where reading the Bible costs lives. Such technology puts teeth to our prayers and complements organizations like Voice of the Martyrs and Bibles Unbound.[13]

Some people are even daring to live in these countries. They are exchanging lives of hot tubs and country clubs for lives of risk and danger. As missionaries, they follow Christ to the ends of the earth and don't look back.

The incarnation was the turning point of history. It split time in two, changed civilization, and showed us that God had planned on getting down and dirty from the beginning of time (Revelation 13:8). It illustrates the depths to which a pursuing God would go to save a rebellious people hitchhiking away from paradise. It teaches us that God cares about our problems—our headaches and heartaches. The American church still has something relevant to contribute to global Christianity, but ordinary people must live radical lives—free of reserve, free of retreat, and free of regret.

"Chocolate is cheaper than therapy,
and you don't need an appointment."

—*Confession of a chocoholic*

5 Chocolate for the Soul

God's Holiness \ˈhōl-ē-nis\

Isaiah never saw it coming. One day he was minding his own prophetic business and God showed up. Above him sat a massive heaviness, complete with a robe that filled an area the size of a building. He might have wet his pants at the sight. "Angel-seraphs hovered above him, each with six wings. With two wings they covered their faces, with two their feet, and with two they flew" (Isaiah 6:2 MESSAGE). What did these creatures need so much protection from?

The white-hot holiness of God. They couldn't even look at God's purity. His brilliance would have fried their faces. His radiation, too toxic. In his book *Not a Safe God*, Tim Riter says, "God is a consuming fire. His nature surpasses ours. He's 220 volts and we're only wired for 12. Experiencing God in His fullness would blow our circuits."[1] These angels couldn't even get close enough to take God's temperature. All they could do was cover themselves and shout, "Holy, Holy, Holy is God-of-the-Angel-Armies" (verse 3 paraphrased).

Holy Places

I've never seen a tornado in person (knock on wood), but they say that if you're close enough it sounds like a freight train passing by. According to meteorologists, an F5 tornado can sustain winds of up to three hundred eighteen miles per hour and can launch an automobile three hundred feet into the air.[2] Anything in its way—houses, minivans, a herd of grazing cows—will be hacked to pieces by projectile shrapnel. It's like getting caught in a blender of razor blades and hammers. Even die-hard tornado chasers armed with bulletproof windows and fancy radar equipment keep their distance from the big ones.

Wherever God spins, His holiness follows. His purity and presence go hand in hand. Throughout the Bible, God's presence at various times took the form of rainbows, fire, or fog.[3] Once, the Israelite priests even had to postpone their worship service because the smoke in the sanctuary was so thick (1 Kings 8:10–11). The prophet Nahum observed, "Tornadoes and hurricanes are the wake of his passage, storm clouds are the dust he shakes off his feet" (Nahum 1:3 MESSAGE). From the dense cloud above Mount Sinai to the burning bush in Egypt, one thing proved true: anytime a holy God intersects with a fallen world, there will always be atmospheric disturbance.

I wrote this chapter barefoot. Not because my Chacos were dirty, but because I am dirty. To stand before God's holiness and try to condense it into twelve pages—well, that's an impossible and rather dangerous thing to do.

When our filthiness meets God's holiness, it's an awful encounter. Plato once said, "We can easily forgive a child who is afraid of the dark; the real tragedy of life is when men are afraid of the light."[4] And we are terrified of it. We're allergic to it. Human beings are creatures of darkness, gremlins who squeal "Bright light! Bright light!" when the lamp is turned on. God's holiness is too beautiful for us to behold. Our pupils are too dilated; our skin, too sensitive. Even with SPF 70 sunscreen we can't approach His melting majesty.

Instead, God approached us. The God who "lives in unapproachable light" (1 Timothy 6:16) flickered to earth as a 100 watt Nazareth bulb. Holiness found a very human place to live. God-with-us became God-is-us. But even then the Light was too strange for us. John wrote, "The light shines in the darkness, but the darkness has not understood it" (John 1:5). It is no surprise that Nicodemus, a Pharisee in the Jewish council, approached the Light of the World in the midnight hour (John 3:2).

• • •

Dark chocolate has long been a delicacy in the world. According to historians, chocolate was the Aztecs' national drink. When Hernan Cortéz came to Mexico in 1519, he observed that Aztec emperor Moctezuma finished every meal with a large shot of liquid chocolate served in a golden goblet with a golden spoon.[5] The Aztecs also incorporated chocolate into their worship services. Not only did they baptize their babies in it and drink it at wedding ceremonies, they also offered it to their gods.[6] Every Aztec warrior was supplied with tablets of ground cacao to use as portable sacrifices before going into battle. With their instant chocolate packages, an ordinary plot of jungle could become a holy place of worship.

The love affair with chocolate continued in South America. In 1620, Thomas Gage reported that in southern Mexico a group of women were so addicted to chocolate that they kept falling asleep in church without it. So when the priest discovered that hot chocolate was being smuggled into the service, the women were punished and excommunicated.[7]

What does it mean to be holy? Holiness is to be set apart. It's the lone Kit Kat bar in a bucket of Butterfingers. Peter wrote, "Let yourselves be pulled into a way of life shaped by God's life, a life energetic and blazing with holiness. God said, 'I am holy; you be holy'" (1 Peter 1:14–15 MESSAGE). Peter knew something about holiness. Jesus explained to Peter that Satan asked to sift him as wheat (or cacao beans, as the case may be; Luke 22:31). But God didn't let that happen. Instead, it was Christ who purified and washed him. It was Christ who filtered and sifted him. But Peter said, "Lord, you don't need to wash my feet."

Holiness is the lone Kit Kat bar in a bucket of Butterfingers.

Jesus replied, "Unless I wash your feet you can have no part in me."

Peter thought for a moment. "Then, Lord, don't just wash my feet. Run me through the car wash!" (John 13:4–9, my own retelling). Peter stumbled upon a very important truth that day: When God calls us to be holy, He always equips us for holiness.

Purity is not a popular theme in our culture. It's ridiculed and grossly misunderstood. Yet God is not going to present Christ with a blemished bride. He is in the holiness business—the harvesting business—refining His people and stripping away their blemishes. "Without holiness," wrote the author of Hebrews, "no one will see the Lord" (Hebrews 12:14). And one day we will see Him face-to-face. On that day we will be altogether holy, as Christ is.[8]

Holy Paces

Holiness is a gradual process. Unlike righteousness, it takes time. The moment we give our lives to God, we are instantly made right with Him. Christ's purity is superimposed over our guiltiness, and we're as perfect and flawless as Jesus.

But holiness is a different beast altogether. John Owen said that holiness is "continually to be renewed and gone over again, because of the remainder of sin in us."[9] Holiness is the morning by morning commitment to become more like Christ. Paul told young Timothy, "Exercise daily in God—no spiritual flabbiness, please! Workouts in the gymnasium are useful, but a disciplined life in God is far more so, making you fit both today and forever" (1 Timothy 4:7–8 MESSAGE). Humans rigorously resist change. We are creatures of habit, animals of addiction who love the rut of routine. If change must occur, it must be gradual. That's why the most successful rehabilitation programs have so many steps.

Christians are changing all the time. We fight an inward battle, a civil war of the soul, a "holy violence," wrote J. C. Ryle.[10] Paul described his struggle: "What I don't understand about myself is that I decide one way, but then I act another, doing things I absolutely despise" (Romans 7:19, my paraphrase). Yet, in this daily combat, God paces alongside us. He encourages us to keep going, to keep fighting, to keep straining for the finish line.

Grace is the grueling work of a determined God.

Holiness is our work, but it's also God's work. Like paddling a rowboat, Christianity is a movement of cooperation with Christ. We push; God pulls. This is a strange synergism, but step by step, row by row, we forge our way to holiness. We don't give up because God doesn't give up. Grace is the grueling work of a determined God. But we also "work out [our] salvation with fear and trembling" (Philippians 2:12). We hold these in happy tension—a beautiful paradox, resolved only in the infinite mind of God.

Led onward by the encouraging words "For he chose us in him

before the creation of the world to be holy and blameless in his sight" (Ephesians 1:4), we can surrender all that threatens the path to holiness. We can shed our friends who discourage us, our possessions that possess us, and our comforts that dull our sensitivity to the Spirit. Anything that moors us can be severed.

Spiritual disciplines are ancient practices that set our spiritual paces. They keep us from laziness and atrophy. But they require patience and stamina. Richard Foster and Emilie Griffin suggest that spiritual disciplines lead to spiritual formation and "perhaps we could think of spiritual formation as a pattern, a series of concrete actions that will gently move us toward transformation in Christ."[11] Like waves in the sea, we can either resist the disciplines or ride them. The surf is up.

Holy Spaces Silence

When God's holiness meets our humanity, we're muted with humility. After Isaiah saw God's swirling center, he shut his mouth. "I'm as good as dead!" he lamented. "Every word I've ever spoken is tainted" (Isaiah 6:5 MESSAGE). Then an angel swooped down and touched Isaiah's lips with a burning hot coal. It sizzled his tongue, and perhaps he never uttered a careless word again.

The discipline of silence is a natural reaction to God's holiness. When we get a glimpse of who God is, we find that His voice is deeper than our own. His words are worth listening to. But we're not accustomed to silence. We react to it, sometimes violently. Our own silence is an X-ray machine and we don't like what we see—loneliness, emptiness, insecurity. We fill up the hollow moments with noise. We blare the radio, blast the TV, and phone our friends. Why? To avoid the deafening roar within.

Even in our churches, silence is an unwelcome visitor. Though well intentioned, our performance-driven gatherings hush our sensitivity to silence. We drench ourselves with sound. It spills down the stage, irrigating aisles and pooling into pews. It soaks and surrounds every inch of us. The louder the better. And we panic when the microphones stop working. *What if they don't come back on?*

This is one reason so many people are finding refreshment in the monastic traditions. Franciscan, Benedictine, and Cistercian monks splurge in silence every day, realizing the seriousness of worshiping God and the frivolousness of empty chatter. They understand the value of sitting before God, waiting for Him to say the first word. God is always talking but our ears are full of wax. Silence is our Q-tip. Granted, there will always be a place for upbeat, ear-popping praise. But when the ringing stops, when the ramblings cease, we find ourselves alone with the still small voice that whispers, "My presence is enough for you."

In the sixteenth century, monks from Spain introduced chocolate to France and Germany.[12] They taught them how to grow the beans and produce chocolate. One of the most important steps was the fermentation process. After separating the cacao bean from its pod, the cacao was left to bask in the sun for three to seven days. Without this exposure to light, the bean would have a low cocoa butter content and weak flavor. Then the bean was dried, stripped of its shell, and sifted for purity. Naked, raw, and sunburned, the bean was then ground up and made into unsweetened chocolate.

Silence ferments our lives. When we carve out time to lodge and lounge in God's light, we receive the nutrients we need for spiritual vitality. The psalmist said that God "set my feet in a spacious place" (Psalm 31:8). When we dwell in His presence and are exposed to His holiness, as Isaiah was, our desires begin to change. Our thoughts turn upward; our hearts, outward. We begin to notice others and really hear what they have to say. Silence feeds a full-throttle addiction to God. It transforms secular space into sacred space. A boring errand becomes an exciting adventure; a mundane desk job, a throne of grace. Any bush can be a burning bush so long as God shows up. And when He does, we can't stop thinking about Him. We can't stop talking about Him. And out of the silence, the ordinary moments morph into extraordinary encounters with God.

What are some practical ways to incorporate silence in our lives? To begin with, it's important to recognize the danger of distraction. We live in a culture of constant stimulation. We're assaulted by magazine covers and interstate marketing. Our eyes are always being pulled toward ads and billboards. One can easily spend a life consumed with consumerism, floating from product to product, waiting for the next big video game to be released. The appetite for silence is just as important as the practice of silence. But you don't need to take off work or travel to a retreat center to practice this discipline. Spiritual silence can occur anywhere. It's about focusing the heart on hearing God. It's about hushing ourselves—whether in the car, in the shower, or walking through a noisy airport.

Silence is difficult for the body, but it's chocolate for the soul.

Silence is difficult for the body, but it's chocolate for the soul. Researchers report that the polyphenol levels in dark chocolate have been shown to prevent heart disease,[13] and flavanol, a nutrient found in cocoa, stimulates neurovascular activity. In other words, chocolate is good for the head and the heart. It releases endorphins into the bloodstream, reduces the risk of blood clots, and contains as many antioxidants as green tea and blueberries. The Aztecs discovered this long ago and often treated coughs, fever, and childbirth complications with it.[14] Like chocolate, silence caffeinates our Christianity, energizing fizzled faith. It keeps us alert to God's voice and helps us live intentionally—not like driftwood that floats with the current. It propels us into the presence of God.

But silence also releases us to speak. Henri Nouwen wrote, "The word is born in silence."[15] John Michael Talbot buttresses his thought: "Being in God's presence brings us to a silence where it becomes easy to listen. It is by listening that we hear His word, and by hearing His word that we learn again how to speak."[16] But it's not just about being quiet. Most anyone can refrain from speaking. Rather, spiritual silence involves active listening, a straining for God's frequency. It's our satellite aimed at heaven, not to broadcast but to receive. With Samuel we say, "Speak, for your servant is listening" (1 Samuel 3:10). And by listening, we are intimately involved with Christ.

Holy Faces

J. I. Packer observed, "The way to find out what a group of people are really like is to see what they habitually talk about."[17] What do we talk about? We talk about sports, weather, weekends, and trends. We talk about what we're going to eat for lunch today and the incredible steak we had last night. We talk about movies and podcasts, plans and vacations. But we rarely talk about God—His beauty, His ability, His master plan for everything. We detach ourselves from those words because we can't control them. They don't fit into our routine-laced lives. They're too wild and unpredictable. We want a calm God, but instead He's hyper. And when we talk about God's bigness, we're reminded of our smallness.

Voices come in many shapes and sounds. Some are deep and raspy, others soft and shallow. Opera singers train ad nauseam to increase their range. Impersonators spend hours before mirrors to look and sound like Donald Trump or Arnold Schwarzenegger. The human voice is flexible and trainable—we can hum, yell, moan, sigh, and cry. Our voices can be encouraging or destructive. They can help humanity or harm it. Adolf Hitler and Benito

Mussolini were powerful orators—marvelous communicators—yet their voices led millions to the slaughter. The Scriptures prove true: "Words kill, words give life; they're either poison or fruit—you choose" (Proverbs 18:21 MESSAGE). Jesus wasn't lying when He said that we will give an account for every careless word we ever utter (Matthew 12:36).

The Roman orator Cicero was right: "Silence is one of the great arts of conversation."[18] But there comes a time to speak. And when we do, the world will recognize us by our words. To be holy in an unholy society means that even our dialogue should be distinct. "Out of the overflow of the heart the mouth speaks" (Matthew 12:34). If we have new hearts—God-infused hearts—our words will be different. Our very faces will change. After Moses listened to God on the summit of Mount Sinai, the Israelites had to bag his head because his face shined so brightly. People should always be able to see if we've been with Jesus. It should be in our eyes, on our lips, and in our smiles. God's voice should be in our voices.

One way we can use our voices to enhance God's kingdom is by speaking out against oppression, human trafficking, and slavery. In the Aztec Empire, one hundred cocoa beans bought a healthy slave.[19] But slavery didn't die with the passing of early South American empires. In the United States there are more than ten thousand slaves imported from more than thirty countries who are held in captivity and forced to work in hotels, restaurants, and in domestic servitude for little or no pay.[20] Slavery exists in almost every major city in America. It's also a thriving enterprise for millions of people around the world. Over two hundred thousand children are trafficked every year in West and Central Africa,[21] and many of them are forced to work on cocoa farms.

The Ivory Coast produces about 60 percent of the world's chocolate and is no stranger to child labor. Many exploited children are regularly beaten with chains and branches, forced to work twelve-hour days, and given little more than corn paste to eat. Their voices go unnoticed, drowned out by the thirteen-billion-dollar chocolate industry.

But God is listening. He hears every cry from every slave in every country. God hears every growl from every stomach. Their faces are lasered on His mind.

In the United States, we talk about ourselves a lot. Many of us have become so insulated that we've forgotten to focus on those no one looks at. In our urge to emerge or converge, our eyes are locked on mirrors while the world is locked in chains. But things are changing. We're turning our attention off of ourselves—theologically, practically, and missionally. We're becoming vocal about the silent evils around us, the violence and abuse.

Human beings are simultaneously under construction and already built. We're holy and fallen at the same time. When God looks at us, He sees the perfection of Christ. He sees what we will be, along with what we already are. Paul reminds us that we are "sold as a slave to sin . . . what I want to do I do not do, but what I hate I do" (Romans 7:14–15). But there's another ingredient in the stew—freedom. Christ has broken us out of jail, beaten down our slave driver, and given us the freedom to surrender our purest praise. Not the kind of praise the Israelites practiced in the book of Malachi when they mixed crippled animals in their offerings. God doesn't want diluted worship. He wants it straight and strong.

For too long our chocolate has been diluted with spiritual milk. But it's time to return to purity. No more Candy Land Christianity. It's time to ferment in the silence of God's light, to bask in the beauty of His love. It's time for unmixed devotion and adoration. But it's also time to speak up. We are shouting for justice when all the world is quiet. Gerald Reed writes, "God's holiness exudes a sweet aroma, tempts our taste buds, and satisfies our sweet tooth."[22]

When we are satisfied in God's holiness, it affects our actions. When our actions are changed, our worship melts like M&M's in God's mouth, and He is pleased with our praise.

"Bart, with $10,000 dollars, we'd be millionaires!
We could buy all kinds of useful things like . . . love."

—Homer J. Simpson

God's Love \ləv\

There's only one way to eat an oyster—raw and smothered in Tabasco sauce. At least that's how I do it. On a blazing May day in Louisiana, few things soothe the soul like a chilled, slimy oyster. Not to mention the crawfish boils—huge pots of spicy crawfish flung across newspaper-covered picnic tables—a blur of tails and torsos. It's a love feast, and there are plenty of us who love feasting.

An editor once told me that I write too much about food. He was probably right. I usually write on an empty stomach. But the Bible's full of food. The Old Testament is gluttoned with banquets and celebrations, from the angel chef who fed Elijah (1 Kings 19:6) to the appointed feasts commanded by God (Leviticus 23:24). David wrote, "You serve me a six-course dinner right in front of my enemies" (Psalm 23:5 MESSAGE) and God "satisfies the thirsty and fills the hungry with good things" (Psalm 107:9). The rich man found a home in hell for withholding food from hungry Lazarus

(Luke 16), and even Jesus was not silent about the stomach. From the prodigal's homecoming meal to the parable of the wedding banquet, food plays a big part in the unfolding of God's story.

Love à la Carte

The love of God is a delicacy. When we talk about the mysteries of God—His power, bigness, beauty, wisdom, and creativity—we're speaking about His qualities. These are His hands, lips, brain, feet, and muscles. But to speak about God's love is something altogether different. It is to peer into His very heart. Every limb is fed from this organ. God's love permeates God's everything because it is the driving thrust of who He is.

It's the chief advisor of His decisions, the grand designer of His plans. No subject in all the world is as deep or wide as this one. No drill bit can mine it; no tractor unearth it. If we're to dive into the depths of God's love, we'd better have our flashlights ready.

God does not only *have* love; He does not only *demonstrate* love. God *is* love.[1] It's not just in His bloodstream; it's in His being. Love is God's active ingredient. Always has been, always will be. Before humans existed, the love of God burned within the society of the Trinity. It was self-contained and self-satisfying. But then God's love outwardly exploded. He aimed His affection at His creation. The more He made, the more He loved. And the crazy part about it, the mind-blowing part, is that God loved His creatures unconditionally.

We often make God in our own image by superimposing our definition of love over His. We expect God's love to be like our love—selfish. We love because "he's so cute," or "she's loaded with cash." Human love has its benefits, its conditions, and no matter how pure we want it to be, it has become tainted by our sin.

But God's love marches to the beat of His heart, not ours. His love is 100 percent in our corner. He attaches Himself to us even when it doesn't make Him look any better. We are cysts on His shoulder, rebellious and ugly. But God loves us anyway. Not because He has to, but because He wants to. He doesn't discard us; He reforms us.

Why did God choose to love the nation of Israel? It wasn't because of their muscles—they were the weakest. It wasn't because of their potential—they were the most stubborn. For the longest time, they didn't even have a formalized country, a land to live in. As Moses told his people on the plains of Moab, "God wasn't attracted to you and didn't choose you because you were big and important—the fact is, there was almost nothing to you. He did it out of sheer love" (Deuteronomy 7:7).

God's love isn't based on how sexy or smart we are. It doesn't take into account our GPA, how much money we earn, or what family we're from. It doesn't even matter how lovable we are. The dam of God's love is not dependent on the valley beneath it. And when it breaks, we can't help but splash along for the ride.

The New Testament writers struggled to communicate the love of God. The Greek and Roman world couldn't understand God's love because their gods lusted after women and took advantage of mortals. Cupid and Eros often placed women under spells to lure them into sexual activity. Even big daddy Zeus, the chief of all gods, seduced countless goddesses by deceiving and betraying them. Greek and Roman soap operas had no room for a love like God's. So the writers of the New Testament had to employ a rarely used Greek word for love—*agape*—to describe God's love.

There is a great beauty between God's giving and our taking. It's God's prerogative to love us and our responsibility to respond—a holy harmony, a ping-pong between His pleasure and our pardon. God will never serve a ball too hard for us to return. He never offers us a love we cannot handle. Rather, God serves us a medicinal kind of love, a cure for our cancer, a remedy for our AIDS. God doesn't blindly shoot His love in our direction, just hoping that we might accept it. Rather, with the precision of a marksman, God snipes us with His love. No wind can offset it. No distance can prevent it. We have been in the scope of salvation since before the world began, and when God pulls the trigger He never misses a shot.

God loves the little things—the things no one wants.

God has a passion for broken things. He collects, polishes, and perfects them. He loves the little things—the forgotten things—the things no one wants. He takes cracked humans and restores them. He takes Humpty Dumpty hearts and puts them back together again. Nothing is too shattered for His superglue. No one is too broken for His construction crew. Even soaking wet, sushi-eating Jonah discovered that God's love can find anyone anywhere, even in the very depths of the deep.

John Piper wrote, "The saving love of God is God's commitment to do everything necessary to enthrall us with what is most deeply and durably satisfying, namely Himself."[2] God's warehouse is full of damaged goods, and if God commits to mend us with affection, He always comes through.

On the menu of salvation, God's love isn't à la carte. You can't order it alone. It comes with a myriad of side dishes. It comes with soul-deep joy and attitude adjustments. When God loves us, He will keep loving us until His love has perfected us. That's just the way He rolls. God never loves a people without making them whole and holy.

Back in my college art classes, I used a kneadable gum eraser almost as much as I used a pencil. Gum erasers are great for detail work and pulling highlights from charcoal portraits. Unlike most erasers, kneadable erasers are self-cleaning and pliable. To clean them all you do is stretch and knead them like dough. After a few stretches, the pencil stains magically vanish and it looks brand-new.

But we human beings can't clean ourselves. We are tarnished through and through. No matter how good we try to be, we can't expunge the bad inside us. We cannot stretch ourselves or punish ourselves to make us right with God. It's God who takes care of that. The burden is on His shoulders. God washes us in *His* sink with *His* soap. Our detergent is weak, but in His dishwasher, all is made spotless. "Come. Sit down. Let's argue this out," God says. "If your sins are blood-red, they'll be snow-white" (Isaiah 1:18 MESSAGE).

The gospel is a rhapsody in red, a swirling narrative of blood and forgiveness.

The gospel of Jesus Christ is a rhapsody in red, a swirling narrative of blood and forgiveness. And the ending is spectacular. Christ dumps our junk in His trunk and erases our stains. He gives Himself without hesitation or reservation. His radiant intervention woos us and wins us. And because of God's selfless transfer, we flock like moths to the lamp of His love.

Fasting

Godly Grub

So here's a confession: Fasting isn't my discipline of choice. In fact, it's ridiculously difficult for me. I'm a novice at it and even as I type these words, a half-empty box of Cheez-Its sits on my desk, laughing at my inexperience.

But fasting is shockingly biblical. God prescribed it. The Israelites practiced it. And for Jesus, it was not a matter of *if* we fast: He said, "*When* you fast . . ." (Matthew 6:16, italics mine). Throughout the Scripture, God's people fasted on many different occasions: illness, war, forgiveness, humility, danger, and ceremony. For New Testament Christians, fasting was observed corporately and privately, often coupled with prayer. The churches at Antioch and

Galatia observed it, Paul kept it, and throughout the history of Christianity fasting has been a regular and necessary discipline to align one's heart with God.

In an age of Taco Bell and Kentucky Fried Chicken, gluttony wins the day. We medicate ourselves with food and govern our lives around meals. We let our bodies go and our souls drag behind. Did you know that the city of Sodom was destroyed for several reasons, not least of which was gluttony? God said, "Now this was the sin of your sister Sodom: She and her daughters were arrogant, *overfed* and unconcerned; they did not help the poor and needy" (Ezekiel 16:49, italics mine). When was the last time you heard a sermon on gluttony? My high school PE coach, Jeremiah Castille, used to say that a lazy body usually reflects a lazy soul.[3] If our physical lives are undisciplined, our spiritual lives are probably rusting too.

By sacrificing food we feast on Christ.

Fasting returns to God the worship we offer to food. In our food-saturated culture, I believe it's the single most neglected discipline. And the most needed, too. In my own limited experiences, fasting exposes my strenuous death grip on the things of this world. It's teaching me to reevaluate my priorities and how I spend my energy. It's showing me that I need to depend on God more than I depend on myself.

Richard Foster wrote, "Fasting is feasting!"[4] By sacrificing food we feast on Christ. We surrender earthly nourishment for godly grub, and by saying "no" to our stomachs and "yes" to our spirits, we're trusting God to satisfy us with Himself. Jesus said, "You're blessed when you've worked up a good appetite for God. He's food and drink in the best meal you'll ever eat" (Matthew 5:6 MESSAGE). Fasting is food for the soul, and if we're not fasting, we're starving ourselves to death.

There are a million reasons not to fast. It's difficult to do, few are doing it, some think it's weird or monkish, there are health and energy concerns, etc. But to experience the presence of Christ through fasting is a reward too exhilarating not to experience. We say to God, "For the next three days, I abandon myself to you. I empty my mind, heart, soul, and stomach so that you can fill me, and thrill me." Fasting weans us from the world by removing the frivolous and the fluffy from our lives. It pulls us into the center of who God is and what He requires of us. It helps us think clearly about our purpose on this planet. And it dethrones our selfishness by making us sensitive to the subtle activities of the Holy Spirit.

How do you fast? Here are some steps that have been of help to me. Pray about it and prepare for it. Fasting is a portal through which God communicates His will, and to enter that environment unprepared is not just risky but altogether dangerous. Drink liquids. Throughout the Bible, fasting often involved a separation from food, not water. After forty days and nights of fasting in the wilderness, Jesus "was hungry" (Matthew 4:2). The body can function without food, but water is a must.

Read and meditate on the Bible during a fast. Passages you've heard a hundred times sprout new meanings, and God uses His Word to speak intimately to us during these times.

Finally, don't make a big deal about it. Jesus told His disciples, "When you practice some appetite-denying discipline to better concentrate on God, don't make a production out of it. It might turn you into a small-time celebrity but it won't make you a saint" (Matthew 6:16 MESSAGE). Fasting is an inward and upward discipline, not an outward one. The motive behind a fast is just as important as the fast itself. We don't fast to get skinny or look pious. We don't fast to punish ourselves or earn God's grace. We fast because it caters us into the nourishing presence of Christ.

Food is not the only substance we can fast from. In a culture that is obsessed with entertainment, a digital fast is a refreshing way to return to God the glory we offer to the Internet, television, movies, video games, and electronics. A digital fast is a temporary abstinence from all digital entertainment for the purpose of growing closer to Christ. Electricity has revolutionized our world for the better, but it has also become an all-consuming god.

Anything that distracts us and threatens to take God's place can be put in its place by fasting. In fact, anything that competes with God *should* be taught a lesson. By doing so we learn to be better students. We learn to keep God's voice the loudest in our lives, to drown out all other frequencies. Most of us are kindergarten Christians, finger-painting with a faith that is undisciplined and inexperienced. But fasting grows us up. It keeps our focus on the Teacher and helps us see what God is writing on the board.

Love Feasts Remembered

In the first century, Christian worship centered on singing, praying, reading Scripture, preaching, and eating. The love feast, also known as the agape, played an important role in Christian homes. While not usually observed today, the love feast is mentioned throughout the New Testament. Luke records that the Christians in Jerusalem "followed a daily discipline of worship in the Temple followed by meals at home, every meal a celebration, exuberant and joyful, as they praised God" (Acts 2:46). Jude also mentions these meals when he described certain godless men who were mingling with the Christians: "These people are warts on your love feasts as you worship and eat together" (Jude 12 MESSAGE).

Where did this feast find its origin? The night before Jesus was arrested, He shared a meal with His disciples. It was His last supper, His final farewell to the men who had spent three years following Him. At the end of the supper, Jesus broke the bread. "This is my body, given for you," He said. "Eat it in my memory" (Luke

22:19 MESSAGE). He did the same with the cup, reminding them of the blood "poured out for you." The Eucharist (literally "giving thanks for God's grace and blessing") took place in the context of a meal, and it's no surprise then that Christians during this time were accused of cannibalism.

Apologist and church leader Tertullian (AD 160–225) described the love feasts in his time as acts of charity toward the poor. "In these feasts, therefore, we testify our love towards our poorer brethren, by relieving their wants."[5] Similar to Old Testament peace offerings, these meals provided for those who could not provide for themselves. In the mid-third century, however, love feasts were separated from the Eucharist, rarely to surface again.

Kung Pao Christianity

But a new day has arrived. Perhaps it's time to reinstate the love feast in our homes, churches, and communities. What would happen if Christians of different denominations and traditions gathered monthly to celebrate a meal in which God was the sole subject of the conversation? Not the news, or the MVP of the game, or the creaminess of the mashed potatoes, but Christ—the ultimate conversation starter. Would this transform our communities? Would it spark revival in our cities?

In the first century, Christians wrote meditations for this meal and read them during the feast. Everyone contributed something to this event, whether a prayer, a reading from the Psalms, or even the singing of a hymn. Modern-day love feasts would add sinews to the skeleton of American Christianity. Every denomination has an emphasis they've become known for. Some highlight worship, others preaching and teaching, spiritual gifts, the Eucharist and sacraments, evangelism, discipleship, or missions. Every church takes most of these seriously, but each tradition has its own forté. Every one of us has so much to contribute, so much to teach, and also so much to learn. We must stand together as a witness to the world that unification is more important to us than deterioration.

There are many taste buds on God's tongue. His palette is planet-wide. John wrote, "For God so loved the *world*" (John 3:16, italics mine). He doesn't just enjoy American burgers and fries; He likes other food, too. God eats Indian curry, Chinese noodles, and Mexican enchiladas. He's no stranger to Belgian waffles, kung pao chicken, fish and chips, and spaghetti with meatballs. If God's never had a snowball from New Orleans, I recommend the jumbo Dreamsicle, heavy on the condensed milk.

The Lord's Supper is a sacred meal. In it we remember His body and blood. We recall with millions of Christians throughout history the love that opened the veins of Christ. We remember that moment when even the sun had to put on its shades because it couldn't stare directly at God's love. Indeed, it was a gory glory, a once-and-for-all event. When God purchased us, He didn't keep the receipt. The Eucharist reminds us of that.

But it also reminds us to be serious about our faith. The presence of Christ is thick at the Lord's Supper, so to speak. And this meal is not merely symbolic, it's significant. Christ *really* shows up to nourish us with Himself. His love and companionship spill from the cup. His brokenness falls like crumbs from the bread.

The Lord's Supper calls us to remember, but it also urges us to await. We await the day when Christians everywhere will eat and worship in a land where division is taboo. In that age, God's love will ultimately be unraveled.

I don't know if they'll have raw oysters in heaven, but Jesus once said all believers will gather there for a great love feast: "People will come from east and west and north and south, and will take their places at the feast in the kingdom of God" (Luke 13:29). God's table has many chairs, and one day Christians will eat together.

Paul wrote, "And now these three remain: faith, hope and love.

But the greatest of these is love" (1 Corinthians 13:13). Why is love greater than faith and hope? Faith involves the present. Hope involves the future. But love transcends time. Love existed before anything existed. In heaven, faith will be sight and hope will be history. But love endures forever. Love needs no casket because it has no funeral.

Salvation is a sticky story, a messy manuscript, but it's also a lovely one. Love is the bond that glued God to humanity. It adheres us to holiness. And nothing can pry apart what God has welded together.

"No other gods, only me."

—God (Exodus 20:3 MESSAGE)

7

Jealous Is My Name

• • •

God's Jealousy \jel-ə-sē\

My mom recently bought two runt teacup Chihuahuas—Penny and Valentino. Together they'd make a poor meal for a hungry cat, but their little faces and tiny grunts can melt a heart of stone. They're small enough to put in your pocket, and to be honest, I've had guinea pigs bigger.

Every once in a while, one of the dogs will get extremely jealous of the other. When Valentino plays with Squeaky Duck, Penny pounces on her brother and claims it as her own. It's not that she likes Squeaky Duck—Squeaky Duck barely squeaks anymore—it's just that she doesn't want Valentino to have it. As punishment, Penny usually takes a "time-out" in the shoebox she's too small to jump out of.

Jealousy is not just limited to miniature rat-dogs. It's in our bloodstream, too. Joe was my best friend growing up. He lived four houses down from me and we spent most of our summers catching snakes in his creek, playing Nintendo (the original Mario Brothers), and kicking the soccer ball in his yard. One day, Joe and I came home from school and right there in the middle of his driveway was a decked-out, freshly painted go-cart. Jealousy became me. It poured out of my pores. For the next two years I begged my parents to buy me a go-cart. I cried for one. I whined for one. Who knows, I might have even sold my soul for one. Jealousy became my middle name, and I spelled it every day.

It's a pleasant thing to talk about the love of God. To speak of His friendship and covenant with us. We enjoy His gentleness and tenderness, coupled with a good glass of lemonade. But God's jealousy makes us squirm. It makes us uncomfortable to think that God takes backseat to no one. We live in a pluralistic society where there are many gods, and any god that claims to be the only God is disregarded.

Don't Mess with God

But God doesn't play second fiddle. He never has and He never will. When it comes to His centrality, God doesn't mess around. Moses said, "God, your God, is not to be trifled with—he's a consuming fire, a jealous God" (Deuteronomy 4:24 MESSAGE). If we play around with that fire, we're going to get burned. God's people learned this the hard way.

When Moses climbed up to talk with God on Mount Sinai, the Israelites created a golden calf out of melted jewelry. They danced around it and sacrificed animals to it. They even declared that it was the god who brought them out of slavery in Egypt. Needless to say, God got mad in a hurry. When Moses came down to the camp, the party came to a halt. He threw down the calf, burned it with fire, ground it to pieces, and forced the Israelites to drink it in water. They learned that the jealousy of God is no silly subject.

The love of God does not negate the wrath of God. His emotions swing both ways. God's justice and holiness are just as important as His kindness and compassion. If we neglect one, we diminish the other. "The Lord, whose name is Jealous, is a jealous God" (Exodus 34:14 MESSAGE). He's jealous of our time, our affections, and our worship.

It is a serious thing to jilt a jealous God.

Why does God get to be jealous and we can't? Because God is at the top of the food chain. Simple as that. We may not like it, but human beings were created "a little lower than the angels" (Psalm 8:5 NKJV). We're higher than insects and animals, but in the grand scheme of things humans are not at the top.

God is. He has a right to be jealous because He is the sovereign Creator. When we place our gods on His throne, His face gets red with rage. God doesn't take rivalry lightly. He wants our loyalty and when we betray Him, rebel and dethrone Him, we're disrespecting His holiness. He may love us, He may forgive us, but at the end of the day, God will be the One on top. It's His way or the highway. And *that* road doesn't lead to heaven.

Hell? Yeah!

These days it's unpopular to believe in hell. We reserve hell for profanity, but not for reality. The concept seems so medieval and old-fashioned. It doesn't sit well with our system. Hell has actually become a laughing matter, something to chuckle about on *South Park* or *The Simpsons.* Jim Carrey summed it up with, "Maybe there is no actual place called hell. Maybe hell is just having to listen to our grandparents breathe through their noses when they're eating sandwiches."[1]

Personally, I don't like to write about hell. It would be easy for me to delete this section and compromise on the topic—writing about hell certainly doesn't help a book's marketing. I don't like hell because it doesn't seem loving or merciful. It doesn't seem kind or compassionate. Statements like this one from John Michael Talbot are difficult to digest: "We can either turn to the fire of God and live, or we can turn to the fire of hell and die."[2]

If I were God, I'd do it differently. Instead of eternal torture in a celestial oven, I think I'd go another route—maybe annihilation or reincarnation. Or perhaps I'd create humans without nerves. Neurobiologist Thomas Park at the University of Illinois at Chicago recently discovered that the hairless, bucktooth mole rat living in East Africa can't feel pain.[3] Turns out, the rodents are insensitive to acid and burning sensations. If I were God, maybe I'd make us all naked mole rats living in dark, painless tunnels.

In our "don't offend me" society, hell is taboo.

But the problem is that I'm not as holy as God. Sin doesn't bother me like it bothers God. In fact, I've become rather comfortable with white lies and dark secrets. But God has a zero tolerance policy for the stuff. In our relativistic culture, where every road leads to God, and who are you to tell me otherwise, we've become too sophisticated for hell. We've outgrown the idea like a bad case of asthma. We've coughed up the notion and thrown away the concept. Do we really think that human beings could spend eternity crisping for their crimes against the Creator?

Jesus thought so. So did the apostles, the martyrs, the church fathers, and, well, basically every orthodox Christian who has ever lived in the last two thousand years. But now, in our "don't offend me" society, hell is taboo. It's understandable. One reason I switched from a landline to a cell phone is because I was sick of telemarketers pushing their products on me. In the same way, we resist those who push religious agendas, and there's certainly an agenda attached to belief in hell.

Yet Jesus spoke more of hell than of heaven. If He included the idea in His missional way of living, so must we. If Jesus was brave enough and honest enough to tell the *whole* story, so can we. As Christians, our mission is simple: "Go everywhere and announce the Message of God's good news to one and all. Whoever believes and is baptized is saved; whoever refuses to believe is damned" (Mark 16:15–16 MESSAGE). God's light goes hand in hand with His heat. And because of that I'm forced to say, "Hell? Yeah!" If hell really exists, it would be the cruelest thing in the world to keep it a secret.

Sin is another word evaporating from our churches. It's not because we doubt the evilness of humanity. Ten minutes of CNN or a quick skim through a history book reveals our wickedness. We don't like the word because it implies our guilt. Being guilty is a negative feeling, and we're encouraged to think positively about ourselves.

A sinless sermon is the quickest way to get a monster crowd.

Sin requires punishment and judgment. It demands a jury and a verdict. By doing away with sin altogether we can make one another feel good about ourselves. By focusing on the positive things—the highly humanistic things—people won't feel uncomfortable and we can pack so many people in our churches that it looks like we have a healthy congregation. A sinless sermon is the quickest way to get a monster crowd.

The Appeal of the Prosperity Gospel

But it is poisoning our people. Health only comes from understanding sickness. The prosperity gospel articulated by many influential preachers says we're already healthy. Its Peter Pan premise is simple: God wants you to be happy, healthy, and wealthy, so think good thoughts and you'll fly to God. It's a Krispy Kreme Christianity that's sweet on the outside but hollow on the inside. In our money-driven culture, the prosperity gospels prevail. It's easy to get speaking gigs with that message. But the real tragedy, the heart-breaking reality, is that in third-world countries it's spreading like wildfire. People are starving for the real story of God, and what do we read them? A lullaby of luxury. When has buying a faster car or wearing a nicer suit ever drawn anyone closer to Christ?

Many of us have an honest question for this sweeping movement: If God wants us to be rich, why wasn't Jesus rich? Jesus was born of a peasant mother in a filthy stable in an unimportant town. He was smuggled to Egypt, worked as a carpenter's assistant, and hung out with fishermen, lepers, and prostitutes. He had no home, few possessions, couldn't pay His taxes, was deserted by His followers, humiliated and stripped, flogged with a whip, nailed to a tree, laughed at, spit on, beat up, hung out to dry, and raised up to die. Sounds like a gospel of poverty, not prosperity, to me. "Go sell whatever you own and give it to the poor," Jesus told the rich man. "All your wealth will then be heavenly wealth" (Mark 10:21).

Like a dirty window, the prosperity gospel blocks an authentic view of Christ. But we're reaching for the Windex. Oswald Chambers said, "The destined end of man is not happiness, nor health, but holiness."[4] It's holiness that satisfies the hardworking dad in India who makes two hundred dollars a year—not the keys to a fully equipped Lexus. It's holiness that comforts the destitute mom in Kenya who just lost her baby to AIDS—not daily spa treatments and luxurious aromatherapy massages.

True prosperity is a life totally surrendered and rendered to God. It's the refreshing life, the life heroic enough to proclaim, "Repent or perish." No more prancing around the gospel. No more avoiding the core of Christianity—God's eraser is stronger than man's Sharpie. We believe in hell because Jesus believed in hell, and we love our friends enough to tell them the truth. An honest life does not shy away from the hard stuff. As actor Leslie Nielsen said, "The truth hurts. . . . Oh sure, maybe not as much as jumping on a bicycle with the seat missing, but it hurts!"[5]

Vow Making

Responding to a Holy God

What goes through our minds when we think about vows? Perhaps marriage—the unconditional promises between a guy and his girl, "in sickness and in health, for richer or poorer, till death do us part." Maybe we think of monastic vows and lifelong commitments to obedience, poverty, and chastity. Vows have played important roles in the development of civilizations. Fifty years ago there was a thriving tradition in northern Albania where a virgin woman could take a vow to become a man. Based on the *Kanun* code of ethics, this vow allowed women to work, dress, and function as men in society. Today, these women, *virgjinesha*, are few and far between and the practice is dying out. But it testifies to the power that vows can have in a culture.

Oaths are as old as dirt. The Israelites took them very seriously. Moses said, "This is what the Lord commands: When a man makes a vow to the Lord or takes an oath to obligate himself by a pledge, he must not break his word but must do everything he said" (Numbers 30:1–2). Oaths are unconditional promises to God. For example, David said that he would not sleep until he found a resting place for the ark of the covenant. Biblical vows, on the other hand, are conditional: "If God does this for me, then I will do this for Him." A vow is motivated by a holy God's graciousness to us, often in times of danger. The vow "provides a tangible means of relating to God, requesting from God and giving to God."[6] Jacob promised that if God provided traveling mercies for his journey, then he would build a memorial stone to remember God's goodness (Genesis 28:20–22).

Vow making is a discipline in response to a holy God. Making a vow and taking an oath are both modern disciplines that can be practiced by Christians of all ages and stages of life. Our promises should be specific and personal. Instead of vaguely vowing to pray or fast more, a better promise to God would be waking up at 6:30 a.m. to spend twenty minutes praying for persecuted Christians in North Korea. Or spending Friday's lunch hour alone with God in the park. These are specific promises that can be accomplished. It also helps to write our oaths on paper and stick them to mirrors so whenever we look at ourselves, we remember to fulfill our commitments to God.

When we commit ourselves to His ways, our desires merge into His desires.

Humans are in the self-preserving business. We cushion ourselves with comforts. Safety nets like airbags and traveler's checks give us a sense of protection. It's in our nature to look out for number one. But the discipline of making oaths and vows keeps us from living for ourselves. It gives us a freedom to deny ourselves and live for others. When we make a promise to God we are obligated to fulfill it. It is our contract with Christ, and until it is satisfied, we're in debt to Him.

In an age of high-interest credit card debt, when American consumerism is more than two trillion dollars in the hole,[7] we react against anything that obligates us. We want independence from debt, from collection agencies, from car payments and anything that claims us. Spiritual obligation is no exception. God commands us to give 10 percent of our income as a tithe to His church, not to mention offerings (anything beyond 10 percent). But that doesn't come very easily to us. We think our finances belong solely to us because we earned them. But we forget that God's daily grace, His sustaining provision, keeps us healthy and safe enough to work.

Vows remind us that God owns everything, including our incomes. With freedom comes responsibility and with responsibility comes obligation—to help the poor, enhance God's kingdom, and share God's spoils with those in need. When we yield ourselves to this reality, we find peace in knowing that God's jurisdiction takes care of all our needs. When we commit ourselves to His ways, our desires merge into His desires. Our wills yield to His will. And the more we practice the discipline of making oaths and vows, the more we decrease as God increases in us.

There is a serious side to vow making. Throughout the Bible, grave consequences were in store for those who failed to fulfill their vows to God. Just ask Samson. He's the first person in the Bible to take a Nazarite vow (*nãzîr* comes from the Hebrew root meaning "to separate," and his vow included abstaining from haircuts, wine, and having contact with the dead). In return, God gave Samson superman strength. He mauled lions with his bare hands. He took out a whole army with the jawbone of a donkey. He was untouchable.

Until he touched Delilah, that is. When Delilah had his head shaved, Samson's strength dissipated. No longer could he manhandle the Philistines. Instead, they gouged out his eyes and stripped away his dignity. He was forced to work as a prisoner and eventually committed suicide in one of their pagan temples. To break a vow is to gain a curse. Before making a promise to God, we should consider the cost of breaking it.

One of the great benefits of this discipline is that oaths and vows help us destroy the lingering sin in our lives. When we volunteer ourselves to God, we're on His clock, not ours. We're doing His business, not ours. Playtime on God's time is no misdemeanor, and vows remind us who we work for.

They also suppress appetites that distract us from God's presence. As strong and independent as we'd like to be, every one of us is susceptible to sin. If the right temptation comes along at the right time in the right way, we're dangerously vulnerable. Paul said, "No test or temptation that comes your way is beyond the course of what others have had to face. All you need to remember is that God will never let you down; he'll never let you be pushed past your limit" (1 Corinthians 10:13). Our problem, however, is that we limit our limits. We're too quick to indulge our temptations and we often give up without a fight.

The more we feed our sins, the hungrier they grow. The more we yield to them, the faster they approach us. We must slay our sins before they slay us. They can't be coddled, cuddled, nurtured, or made to feel at home. If we play around with sin, it will play around with us—and sin plays rough. We must starve it, hate it, deprive it, and destroy it. In the psalms, Asaph had such a recognition of his sin that he told God, "I was a brute beast before you" (Psalm 73:22). Without the taming power of grace we're like werewolves, unable to control our monstrous tendencies. And the moon is rising.

Christians make oaths with God, but God also makes oaths with us. After Noah's generation provoked God's waterlogged wrath, a rainbow circled the sky, reminding mortals of God's oath never to destroy the world again with water. In another instance, God promises that He will not break the bruised reed (Isaiah 42:3). This is a strange statement to American ears, but if you go to the Nile River today you can see thousands of reeds growing on its shores. The ancient Egyptians used them to make papyrus paper, but bruised or bent reeds couldn't be cut into even strips. They were useless and eventually destroyed.

God loves the stepped on. The mistreated are His masterpieces.

But God preserves His plants. No one is too poor or lowly for His love. He is so pregnant with mercy that He protects the bruised and the bent over. He loves the stepped on and the looked over. The mistreated are His masterpieces. There were times in Jesus' ministry when huge crowds followed Him. Sometimes He would preach to them, other times He'd heal their sicknesses. But sometimes He must have just looked at them and hurt for them. They were all alone in this world, flocking together like sheep. Exposed to demons and illness, clinging to anything and everything that promised healing and hope. When Jesus asked His disciples, "Do you also want to leave?" Peter responded, "Lord, to whom shall we go?" (John 6:67–68).

There was no one else but Christ. No one to comfort them, no one to save them. It makes sense for Christ to weep over Jerusalem. It makes sense that God would write His best poems on those reeds, those broken branches. It makes sense that God would be pleased to bruise His Son for their salvation (Isaiah 53:10).

Master Composer

Saxophone players know a lot about reeds. To produce a good raspy sound, air's got to travel between the reed and the mouthpiece. There are many thicknesses of reeds, and a correct embouchure (tightness of the mouth around the reed) regulates how strong the vibrations are.

Christians are God's mouthpieces. Peter wrote, "If anyone speaks, he should do it as one speaking the very words of God" (1 Peter 4:11). Bruised and cracked as we are, God puts us in His mouth so we can speak His truth. He attaches us to His mouthpiece by the ligature of His love and God's embouchure won't let us slip away. It's not our strength that makes the sound; it's God's breath. It's His lungs that make the gales, and when God blows, He mesmerizes the world with His music.

Jesus promised to give His disciples words when they needed them (Luke 21:15). But He also gives us songs (Job 35:10). Music is an outward expression of God's jealous singularity. God wants His tune on our tongues. He wants His melody in our ears.

Johann Sebastian Bach is considered by many to be the greatest classical musician ever to have lived. Mozart, Beethoven, and Chopin praised him and at times wouldn't begin to compose a song before listening to Bach's recent work. Over the course of his lifetime, Bach wrote a thousand pieces of music, and nearly 75 percent of them were for use in God's worship.[8]

Bach took his Christianity as seriously as his compositions. He enjoyed exegeting biblical passages with music and always signed his works with the initials S.D.G.—*Soli Deo Gloria* (to the glory of God alone). Bach recognized God as the Master Composer and when he played, he worshiped. When Bach was forty-eight years old, he received a copy of Martin Luther's German translation of the Bible and devoured it. In the margins of 2 Chronicles 5:13, which talks of musicians praising God, Bach inscribed, "At a reverent performance of music, God is always at hand with His gracious presence."[9] Jaroslav Pelikan suggested, "According to Bach, the highest activity of the human spirit was the praise of God, but such praise involved the total activity of the Spirit."[10]

We don't have to be Bach to please the Lord with sound. We don't have to play an instrument or compose a cantata. We don't need perfect pitch or whole-tone vibrato. The psalmist declared, "I will sing to the Lord, for he has been good to me" (Psalm 13:6). God receives glory when we are so overcome by His presence that noise escapes our lips even when we try to contain it.

It's easy to let the world set the tempo for our lives. All we have to do is nothing at all. We just have to get out of bed and let society mandate our attitudes for the day—let commercials convince us we don't have enough products and sitcoms set the bar for what's funny or moral. But drummers know what happens when they listen to the crowd instead of the song—they get off beat. That's why many drummers wear earplugs when they're playing so they can mute out the background noise.

Never in history have Christians needed headphones more than now. We've become so melded to the world's mentalities that it's difficult to tell where Christianity begins and secularity ends. God's song is so faint that whatever happens to be on the radio drowns it out. And all the while our true love, our first love, is forgotten.

We don't just go to church to get our God-fix. We go to church to fix our eyes on God.

Worse, with some buttered popcorn and a ticket, our modern church worship could pass for anything the entertainment industry has to offer—the lights, the sounds, the seamless transitions from performance to performance. These aren't inherently wrong, but they do reflect our desire to look, act, think, talk, and entertain as the world does. It takes a forensic expert to locate the microscopic traces of God in some of today's Christian music. But we don't just go to church to get our God-fix. We go to church to fix our eyes on God. And the whole world is watching our watching.

Every generation has a name: the silent generation (1925–1945), the baby boomers (1946–1964), generation X (1965–1980), and the millennial generation (1981–2000). Names define us, but we also define our names. Being named *Christian* has been a burden and a blessing. It's certainly a hard name to live up to. Every time someone calls me by my name, I'm immediately reminded of who and whose I am. There's no escaping it. My most convicting moments have been when people simply asked me my name at parties, clubs, or other crazy places I had no business being at.

We know that we can never articulate every aspect of God, but we're learning to see the beauty of His names. Each name describes a quality of God that fixes our thoughts on Him. For instance, *Elohim* means "Creator, Preserver, Transcendent, Mighty." *El Shaddai* means "God All Mighty." *Adonai* means "Master, Lord." *Magen* means "Shield." *Shaphat* means "Judge." *El-Olam* means "Everlasting God." *El-Berith* means "God of the Covenant." Like a high-quality diamond, every aspect, cut, and color of God excites us. Every facet is fascinating.

True prosperity is peace with God. It's not found in riches, health, or applause. It's not in how the world perceives us. God's approval is what we seek, not man's. His ovation is our desire. The Scottish Reformer John Knox was once told, "Mr. Knox, the whole wide world is against you." To this he responded, "And I am against the world." We can agree with Paul, "What the world calls smart, God calls stupid" (1 Corinthians 3:18 MESSAGE).

When our spirituality spills into every part of our lives, we become a God-intoxicated people. Regardless of our jobs, we can sign God's initials on our work. Whether we design websites, construct houses, prosecute criminals, or sell electronics, everything we do can reflect what God has done and is doing in us. We are ready for a divine detox—a purging of all that is not Christ in us. We're ready for disciplines that suck the secular from our bloodstreams. We can win the world for God not by merging with it or emerging from it, but by transforming it with the power and clarity of the gospel of Jesus Christ.

It's a scandalous salvation, that God would die so we can dare to live. But it's a scandal worth circulating. Like a symphony, the message of hope makes for some marvelous music—some funky jazz faith. And when we learn to hum that hymn, to sing *that* song, to live *that* way, the world will sing along.

"Just because the tomb is empty
doesn't mean our minds must be also."

—*Timothy George*

8 Inbox (1)

• • •

God's Wisdom \wiz-dəm\

The weighty wisdom of God can't be fathomed with ink. It can't be plastered to paper or bound to leather. His brain is too big; His mind, too monstrous. To speak of God's wisdom is to admit our ignorance. And God's foolishness is smarter than all of man's scholarship.

Paul wrote, "God's secret wisdom [is] a wisdom that has been hidden" (1 Corinthians 2:7). But before we seek to know the Creator's mind, we first must plumb our own. According to Paul, our minds are fallen organs, corrupted by sin (Ephesians 4:23). That means no matter how much we think we know, our knowledge is limited in its ability to maintain perfect thought.

Postmodernism recognizes this. We recognize the limitations of human logic to prove the existence of God. A God who must be proved is a God who must be pitied. But Art Hoppe did have a point: "If there's no God, who pops up the next Kleenex?"[1] We're becoming okay with the idea that there's more to this world than just the physical. There's more to life than meets the eye. Something must meet the soul. And though the pendulum of postmodernism often swings so far as to deny truth altogether, at least we're aware of our intellectual inabilities.

But God's thoughts are not our thoughts. The psalmist agreed: "Your thoughts—how rare, how beautiful! God, I'll never comprehend them" (Psalm 139:17 MESSAGE). They're beyond us, above, and below us. But they're also before us. We could never reach up and grab them, so God bent down to share them. God discloses His thoughts to us in the Bible. It's our source of truth, our anchor in the sea. When life strikes, it's good to be grounded in God's Word. God gave us minds to redeem them, and He gave us passions to fulfill them. On every page of the Bible these desires are revealed. And they're written on our hearts (2 Corinthians 3:3). Christians are God's diaries. We are God's thoughts, scribbled to skin and bones.

Two men were walking on the road to Emmaus. Suddenly a stranger joined their journey. "What are you guys talking about?" the stranger asked.

One of them, Cleopas, responded, "Are you the only one in Jerusalem who hasn't heard what's happened during the last few days?"

"What happened?"

"The things that happened to Jesus of Nazareth . . . the high priests betrayed Him and had Him killed. But we had hoped that He was the One who would redeem Israel" (Luke 24, my retelling). Then the stranger did something very strange. "He opened their minds to understand the Scriptures" (v. 45). They recognized Him—Jesus of Nazareth—and commented, "Were not our hearts burning within us while he talked with us on the road and opened the Scriptures to us?" (v. 32).

Our knowledge of God begins with God. He is the One who opens our thoughts to His thoughts and teaches us to read His Word. Solomon wrote, "The Lord gives wisdom, and from his mouth come knowledge and understanding" (Proverbs 2:6).

These days, we're pretty biblically illiterate. A hundred years ago if you cut a Christian, he or she often would bleed the Bible. Ancient seminaries even required students to memorize the whole book of Psalms. But today we bleed John Grisham, Stephen King, or that latest chick flick to hit the shelf. We need a blood transfusion. We need to dig again in the Ancient Book, to bathe in the Bible—to soak in the Scriptures to see if it has something to say.

God gives us knowledge to "lead us to higher worship, greater faith, deeper holiness . . ."

According to John Stott, God gives us knowledge to "lead us to higher worship, greater faith, deeper holiness, better service."[2] He gives us wisdom so we can act wisely. But what are our motives for gaining wisdom? Jonathan Edwards wrote, "Seek not to grow in knowledge chiefly for the sake of its applause, and to enable you to dispute with others; but seek it for the benefit of your souls."[3] God gives us insights so we can worship Him in spirit and in truth. A. W. Tozer said, "Worship, I say, rises or falls with our concept of God . . . and if there is one terrible disease in the Church of Christ, it is that we do not see God as great as He is."[4] He gives us wisdom to discern what is worth reading and what is worth discarding.

Absorbing bad theology is like sweating off a junk food high—it's fun for an hour, but then everything crashes. Our concepts of God affect every aspect of our lives. If we view Him as feeble or distant, we won't risk our lives for Him. If we view Him as uninterested or apathetic, we won't waste our time on Him. But if we view God as the Bible portrays Him—able and active, interested and interesting—we discover a God worth wrapping our minds around . . . a God worth wrapping our hearts around.

We need an upside-down way of thinking. One difference between philosophy and theology is that philosophy begins with man and thinks up to God. Theology, on the other hand, begins with God and thinks down to man. When we think upside down instead of down side up, God becomes our starting point. His reality sets the tone for ours. His truth and His holiness direct our own. Only when we begin with God can we end in godliness.

We sometimes see God as a reclining deity, uninvolved in the course of life. We cloak this concept as God's foreknowledge. We say, "Oh, He knows the future, but He's not involved in the present," or "He knew that I would become a Christian, but He didn't have a hand in my conversion." The problem with putting too much weight behind God's foreknowledge is that God isn't bound by time. He doesn't live in the past and merely peer into the future. He is in the past. And He is in the future. Because God is, we are. Because God has been, we will be.

God doesn't learn. He knows. And what does He know? Everything. Every blade of grass that grows, every grain of sand that blows. He calculates the angles of every tree and the weight of every rock. Even falling snowflakes can't hide their naked templates from His gaze. If God understands nature to this extent, how much more does He understand us? Jesus told His disciples, "He pays even greater attention to you, down to the last detail—even numbering the hairs on your head!" (Matthew 10:29–30 MESSAGE)

Meditation

Things Above

What if all your thoughts were uploaded to the Internet? Not just your best thoughts—your world peace or going green thoughts—but all of them: your dirty laundry thoughts, your secret sexy thoughts, everything. What if those were made public to your parents, friends, classmates, and coworkers? Would that change the way you think? Would it change the way you are?

Jesus was a mind reader. "He knew their thoughts" is a common phrase throughout the Gospels. His divine telepathy was always at play. The psalmist was correct, "The Lord knows the thoughts of man" (Psalm 94:11). What a scary thing! That God can see our musings. That even after dark, His night vision captures our cognitions. If there's one thing Christians must adjust, it's our thinking. We must pry our thoughts from the trivial and force them upward. Paul said, "Look up, and be alert to what is going on around Christ—that's where the action is. See things from his perspective" (Colossians 3:2 MESSAGE). If we want to live as Christ lived, we have to think as Christ thought.

The discipline of meditation moves us into the deep and penetrating presence of God. It charts the inner landscapes of the soul and shows us how to adopt the mind of Christ. Like a car, the soul needs regular maintenance. If we fail to pump it gas or change its oil, we're not going to drive very far. Meditation tunes us up.

But it also tunes us in. Meditation syncs us with the Savior in a way that other disciplines don't. Meditation makes the mundane things of life magical. Simple objects become gateways to God. A blade of grass points to God's creativity. A sheet of rock reflects His protection. Even the drippings of a leaky radiator reveal God's ever-flowing love. Meditation focuses our minds on a single subject—a poem, a picture, a leaf, a rusted bicycle wheel—and shows us Christ in the ordinary.

Some people think this discipline is reserved for monks and nuns who have all the time in the world to harvest their interior lives. Others think Eastern religions have the corner on meditation. But Christians can train their minds to think about God, and we should. German pastor and theologian Dietrich Bonhoeffer was asked why he meditates and he responded, "Because I am a Christian."[5] Paul told us to fill our minds with those things that are true, noble, right, pure, lovely, admirable—to meditate on things that are "excellent or praiseworthy" (Philippians 4:8). God has something to tell us—a message in our inbox—and meditation opens our mail.

Engage . . . Observe . . . Apply . . . Meditation is a practice of recovery and discovery.

While there are many ways to meditate on God, here are a few suggestions: Isolate a single object. The simpler the better. Carve out enough time to wrap your mind around it. Engage it, observe it, then apply it. Encounter it with your senses. Touch it with your mind—smell it, feel it, hear it, taste it (lick it if you have to). Attach yourself to your object and make it the center of your moment. Tune out the world; it has distracted you enough today.

A single verse of Scripture is often a perfect subject to start with. You could spend a whole life meditating upon a phrase in the Bible and it wouldn't be a wasted life. Let's say we want to meditate on Psalm 1:3: "He is like a tree planted by streams of water" (NIV). First, engage it. Go to a city park or garden and find a tree planted by streams of water. It doesn't have to be a big tree as long as it meets the specifications of the psalm. Sit beneath it. Touch its bark, enjoy its shade, feel the strength of its branches. Trace it with your eyes. Sketch it with your mind. God can reveal His wisdom through this tree.

Observe it. What kind of tree is it? Where is it planted? Not by a seashore where salt would corrode its roots. Not by a pond, lake, or stagnating reservoir. Instead, your tree is planted by streams of water—refreshing and nourishing. Everything this tree needs has been allocated for by the Gardener. It grows up and spreads out. It grows down and spreads deep.

Finally, apply it. Think about your own life and see if this tree can teach you something about where you came from or where you need to go. Peter wrote, "His divine power has given us everything we need for life and godliness through our knowledge of him who called us by his own glory and goodness" (2 Peter 1:3). The Gardener never plants us where His grace can't sustain us. He doesn't root us to abandon us. Meditation is a practice of recovery and discovery. We recover our purpose in this world and discover God's mercies, new every morning.

We can't grow to God ourselves. In the Middle Ages, some trees tried. The forest of medieval Catholicism insisted that if you take enough pilgrimages to shrines or pray enough to saints, God will be satisfied with your effort and reward you with heaven. But in 1517, a young, stubborn oak named Martin Luther nailed his ninety-five opinions to a wooden door in Germany and started wildfires that over time spread all the way from Europe to North America. Luther was a tree planted by streams of reformation water.

Christians aren't wild trees, growing randomly in the jungle. Every one of us is sown deliberately. We're planted for a purpose. We might become a bench for some or a book for others. Who knows what God will do with you—the people you'll impact, the lives you will touch? Meditation opens us to the informing, reforming, and transforming power of God.

Forests to Enjoy

Aspen willow trees are thoroughly unique. Unlike the pine, for example, aspens share an underground root system that connects them to one another. In other words, they don't grow alone. Underground colonies shoot stems upward from beneath the soil, producing forests of interlaced trees. These colonies can survive for thousands of years, and because of their interconnectedness, aspens can even withstand forest fires. Some colonies in Minnesota are allegedly dated at eight thousand years old.[6]

Books are part of humanity's root system. They connect us to one another by dissolving the barrier of time and distance. The old adage is true—the pen is mightier than the sword (unless you have one of those knife pens—that's the best of both worlds!). I met a pastor once who told me that he only reads one book—the King James Version of the Bible. I liked his sentiment, his emphasis that God's Word is enough. And if I were on a deserted island, the Bible would be my primary book of choice (or maybe *The Worst-Case Scenario Survival Handbook*).

But God has harvested forests of knowledge for us to enjoy. He's cultivated hundreds of Christian authors who have something significant to contribute to our experiences. Every book is unique. Each has its own feel and smell—fat ones, thin ones, red ones, blue ones. Even old-school books like *The Rare Jewel of Christian Contentment,* by Jeremiah Burroughs, and *Remedies for Wandering Thoughts in Worship,* by Thomas Brooks, can refresh our faith. For some reason, I prefer reading dead writers to living ones. They seem to have more to say and can say it better. Of course, you won't find *The Interior Castle* by St. Teresa of Avila on the *New York Times* Best Seller list, but these books can give clarity to our convictions. To read a book is to engage its author—to invite him or her into your living room. In rare cases, authors can stay for a lifetime.

A good library gets me all nostalgic for heaven. Here's my theory: humans were originally planted near trees in Eden, but since we were banished from the garden I suppose the next best thing is a well-tended library—processed trees! Argentine author Jorge Luis Borges said, "I have always imagined that Paradise will be a kind of library."[7] Touché, Jorge.

Meditation isn't limited to libraries. It can occur anywhere.

But if there's one rule that should be followed, it's this: Meditating doesn't allow for multitasking. We shouldn't think about one thing while juggling four other things. God wants us undivided and undistracted. The psalmist said, "Let me understand the teaching of your precepts; then I will meditate on your wonders" (Psalm 119:27). Knowledge of God precedes mediation on God. But meditation on God enhances our knowledge of God. And only when we know God can we truly know ourselves.

Radical Discipleship

On earth, Jesus never wrote a book. He never inserted a footnote or numbered a page. He never proofread a manuscript or edited a galley. Once, He bent over to scribble something in the dirt (John 8:6), but we don't even know what He wrote. Instead of leaving us books, Jesus left us believers. He injected His thoughts, ambitions, values, and lifestyle into twelve men. He taught them how to live and die, how to fish for men and spread the gospel. Jesus ran a discipleship business.

Discipleship didn't originate with Jesus. In early Jewish culture, students often sought rabbis to study under. R. T. France wrote, "Every Jewish teacher worth his salt had a circle of disciples who followed him. . . . Their teacher was the most important person in their lives."[8] In New Testament times, the Greek and Roman world understood the importance of apprenticeships. Socrates surrounded himself with "learners" who absorbed his teaching.[9] In India, upper-caste families enrolled their children in classes taught by gurus. In ancient Chinese cultures, *sifus* taught *ru men*, "one who passed through the door,"[10] the secrets of kung fu.

Yet Jesus introduced a different kind of discipleship. In most ancient forms, students chose their master, but Jesus reversed the trend. Jesus handpicked His disciples, one by one, and called them to follow Him. "You didn't choose me," He reminded them, "I chose you, and put you in the world to bear fruit" (John 15:16).

Unlike Greek and Roman discipleship based on heady knowledge and abstract concepts, Jesus imparted more than cerebral understanding. He transmitted wisdom. Wisdom is the application of information. It's the "what you do" with the "what you know." To hang out with Christ for three years was not an exercise in Jewish debate or brainy accumulation. Instead, Jesus gave them a full body scrub down, a total makeover of body and soul. At the end of *that* education, twelve enlightened men went on to transform the landscape of Western civilization.

Before we can disciple others, Jesus must disciple us.

Discipleship is a radical form of evangelism. "Radical" comes from the Latin *radix*, meaning root. When we practice discipleship, we plant ourselves deeply into the lives of others. It's about the face time, the soul time. It's about letting our contagious Christianity rub off on others—an investment of time and energy. It's an outward demonstration of an upward reality—that God has invested Himself in humanity.

In a nationwide survey, The Barna Group interviewed hundreds of pastors and church leaders about how they measured success. Barna noted, "Not one of the adults we interviewed said that their goal in life was to be a committed follower of Jesus Christ or to make disciples of the entire world—or even their entire block."[11] Eight out of ten people interviewed said that they judged their successes by their families, career developments, and financial achievements.[12]

Jesus was concerned with families, but He also said, "If anyone comes to me and does not hate his father and mother, his wife and children, his brothers and sisters—yes, even his own life—he cannot be my disciple" (Luke 14:26). Jesus was concerned with career development, but He also said, "Did you not know that I must be about My Father's business?" (Luke 2:49 NKJV). Jesus was concerned about finances but also said, "You cannot serve both God and Money" (Matthew 6:24). When Christians exchange the best things for the good things, we miss out on the great things God has in store for our lives.

Before we can disciple others, Jesus must disciple us. Unless our words match His words, we can't teach others to talk. Unless our actions emulate His actions, we can't show others how to live. Out of the heart the mouth speaks, and if God dwells richly in our lives, our lips will reflect our love.

Discipleship requires a life of total conformity to God. It demands a constant awareness of Christ's presence. Dietrich Bonhoeffer said, "Christianity without the living Jesus Christ remains necessarily a Christianity without discipleship; and a Christianity without discipleship is always a Christianity without Jesus Christ."[13] The two go hand in hand.

• • •

Being a Christian is not a mindless calling. When God enters a life, He doesn't hollow out the head. Ours is not a fairy-tale faith in a Hansel and Gretel God. Rather, we believe in Him because the evidence is overwhelming—internally and externally. The trail of breadcrumbs is too compelling; the signs, too obvious. Grace doesn't make us gullible; it makes us pliable. It stretches our thoughts and molds our minds. It realigns our attitudes. It readjusts our inclinations. A faith that doesn't think is a faith that doesn't thrive. Yet thinking about God is not just an academic activity for the brain. The author of the book of James wrote, "Faith by itself, [without] action, is dead" (James 2:17). It involves everything we are—everything we can be. The Puritans used to say, "We ask great things of a great God." So we keep on asking. We keep on learning.

We can question the Bible, but beware; the Bible can question us back. God's Word is samurai sharp, slashing through armor and cutting through pride. It renders us defenseless and vulnerable. But it also helps us fix our thoughts on Jesus (see Hebrews 3:1). Knowing God in all His wisdom is the highest aspiration of the human intellect.

"If anyone would come after me, he must deny himself and take up his cross daily and follow me."

—Jesus (Luke 9:23)

9

Cardboard Crosses

• • •

God's Patience \ˈpā-shəns\

It was just one of those days. You know the kind—endless classes, hours of homework, a headache that Rapid Release Tylenol Gelcaps couldn't even tame. Cartoonist Bill Watterson described it perfectly: "You know, Hobbes," Calvin said, "some days even my lucky rocket ship underpants don't help." It was my last semester of seminary and I was ready for graduation. After three years of Hebrew verbs and student loans, the only thing thinner than my patience was my wallet. And on that particular day, it contained a meager two Mr. Washingtons.

For those who don't mind sticky floors and splotchy screens, the dollar movie theater is good anesthesia for rough days. Of course, if you need to use their bathroom, you just might contract a bacterial disease. And it's always good to pop some vitamin C before you go, just to give your immune system a heads-up. But these were risks I was willing to take. After loading our shirts and pants with gas-station refreshments, my wife, Rebecca, and I strolled into the run-down theater.

Halfway into the previews, several teenage girls sitting to our left started talking. They weren't just whispering, which is somewhat tolerable. They were using their "outside voices." Five minutes of chitchat became fifteen. Fifteen became twenty. As the movie progressed, my composure regressed. Granted, the conversation was quite informative. We learned all about who asked whom to the prom, how he was way out of her league, and where she could go if she ever said that again.

Now I'm told that in situations of this nature it's perfectly acceptable to turn around and politely ask the patrons to lower their voices. But for whatever reason, it didn't come out that way.

"*Shutyourmouths!*" I screamed at the very top of my lungs.

The whole theater flinched. The girls were shocked. "Oh no, he didn't," they whispered. Oh yes he did! My wife sank low in her seat, embarrassed and apologetic. Ten minutes later, the tension was too thick and we left. But not without hearty applause from the cheerleading section.

Unlike me, God is longsuffering. His patience permeates His entire being. David wrote, "But you, O Lord, are a compassionate and gracious God, slow to anger" (Psalm 86:15). The Hebrew literally reads, "God is long of nose." In other words, when God gets ticked off, it takes a long time for His nose to flare in anger. The wick of His temper is skyscraper tall. It takes a ton of sewage to clog His septic tank. Unlike Pinocchio, God always tells the truth, and when He says that He's "endlessly patient" (Exodus 34:6), we can put stock in those words.

God does, however, have a breaking point, a boiling point. But even that isn't a point of no return. He told His chosen people, "In an outburst of anger I turned my back on you—but only for a moment. It's with lasting love that I'm tenderly caring for you" (Isaiah 54:7–8 MESSAGE).

A Vengeful Prophet, a Patient God

The prophet Jonah knew this all too well. He knew that if he preached the Good News to the Ninevites, they might repent. And if they repented, God would exert patience and refuse to destroy them. The problem was, Jonah wanted them destroyed. He wanted them wiped off the face of the earth. Ever since he was a boy, he'd heard horror stories about the cruelty of Assyrian warriors. The Assyrians often cut off the skin of their prisoners and decorated their city walls with it. They enjoyed hacking off noses, plucking out eyes, and making pyramids of human corpses. Assyrians found pleasure in holocaust, yet the God of the Hebrews sought to have mercy on them and sent a prophet their way.

I imagine Jonah didn't preach very loudly when he arrived in Nineveh. He probably slurred his words and mumbled his message. Yet when the sermon reached the ears of the rulers, the king stripped off his clothes and ordered a citywide fast. He mandated that everyone—rich and poor, popular and peasant—beg the God of the Israelites to have pity on them. "Who knows?" the king speculated. "Maybe God will turn around and change his mind about us, quit being angry with us and let us live" (Jonah 3:9 MESSAGE). Though it's not in the Hebrew Bible, ancient Assyrian records reveal this prayer: "I turn to my merciful god and I groan, Lord, reject not thy servant—and if he is hurled into the roaring waters, stretch to him thy hand! The sins I have committed, have mercy upon them! My faults, tear them to pieces like a garment!"[1]

It's an awful thing to meet an angry God. But even the Ninevites, the most savage people in the known world, found patience and mercy in the one true God of Israel. They discovered that God "is patient with you, not wanting anyone to perish, but everyone to come to repentance" (2 Peter 3:9). Eventually, however, Nineveh was destroyed with water. But for that generation, for those who got on their faces and repented, they found forgiveness instead of destruction.

I often wonder how far God's nose has burned when it comes to my country. Fifty years ago it was common for a public school classroom to open the morning in prayer to the Judeo-Christian God, and then recite the pledge of allegiance to the flag of the United States of America. Wow, how things have changed! We now scoff at such a thing. We do everything we can to kick God out of the classroom and out of the government; we shun Him in our public places. The faintest trace of Him results in megadollar lawsuits. Yet God doesn't whine about it. He doesn't make a stink about it. Instead, He does something far worse, far more terrifying—He simply leaves. He complies with our request and gets out of Dodge.

But when a 9/11 or Hurricane Katrina strikes, people immediately ask, "Where was God when this happened?" Suddenly we want Him back, scolding Him for ever leaving. We want Him to shelter us from danger, to spare us from the fate of other civilizations.

As I travel from college to college and church to church, I'm astonished at the grassroots readiness for revival. It can't be categorized or labeled, but we're ready to encounter God in a fresh and authentic way. We need direction, encouragement, and role models. We need people to live what they preach and preach something worth living for.

Throughout history, revival has always been the work of God. He is the One who lights the fire. But spiritual disciplines fan what God has begun. If we acquire an openness to God's leading, there's no telling how He'll use us to enhance His kingdom. What God told Solomon applies to us, too: If "my people, who are called by my name, will humble themselves, and pray and seek my face and turn from their wicked lives, then will I hear from heaven and forgive their sins and heal their land" (2 Chronicles 7:14).

A Heavier Cross

The patience of God found greatest expression on the cross of Christ. It was a moment of reckless carnage—when the cleanest became the filthy. Paul wrote, "Christ never sinned! But God treated him as a sinner, so that Christ could make us acceptable to God" (2 Corinthians 5:21 CEV). Instead of fighting the nine-inch Roman nails, He embraced them. Instead of avoiding the four-inch Jerusalem thorns, He absorbed them.

Richard Foster explains, "Christ not only died a 'cross-death,' he lived a 'cross-life.' "[2] When Jesus felt like losing His temper, He stretched out His arms on the cross. When He felt like quitting, He gave His back to the whip. Jesus always put the Father's agenda before His own. He always surrendered His will to the greater plan. And when He tells us to take up our daily crosses, He speaks as One who was hourly crucified.

I don't know much about dying. Sure, I've seen it on the movies and heard it on the news, but I've never held the hand of a dying patient or held the head of a dying soldier. I'm an amateur at death, and even more so at dying daily. My cross is cut from cardboard, not concrete. It's covered in bubble wrap and equipped with heated massagers. The burdens my faith generates feel like superficial silhouettes of what others carry.

But J. I. Packer suggested, "Christian joy is greatest when the cross is heaviest."[3] A heavy cross—a substantial faith—is a life of purpose and satisfaction. When we take our Christian convictions seriously, our crosses grow heavier. The more we encounter Christ, the more He changes us. The more we change, the less the world understands us. And by living differently from society, people will be drawn to the God who is "slow to get angry and huge in loyal love" (Numbers 14:18 MESSAGE).

• • •

In the box office hit movie *Cast Away*, Chuck Noland (played by Tom Hanks, who was nominated for an Academy Award for his performance) is a FedEx employee who finds himself stranded on a deserted island in the South Pacific. Having worked at a job where time equals money, Noland is now enveloped in a life of solitude and silence. He becomes so lonely that he has to create a friend, Wilson, out of a bloodstained volleyball, just to have someone to talk to. Of course, the island has no taxis, pizzerias, or plumbing; even the simplest items are unavailable. Soon, survival becomes the name of the game—and Noland isn't winning. He can't make a fire, he can't fish worth a flip, and he nearly drowns trying to sail out to sea.

Four years later and fifty pounds lighter, Nolan has adjusted to the primitive way of life. He's now a master fisherman, and later he builds a boat that eventually floats him to his rescuers.

When he finally returns to the hustle and bustle of the world he left, his outlook on life is different. He doesn't live by the clock anymore. He appreciates the little things of life—the illumination of a lightbulb and the texture of an ice cube. "And I know what I have to do now," he tells a friend. "I have to keep breathing. Because tomorrow the sun will rise. Who knows what the tide could bring?"[4]

By Quiet Waters Solitude

The discipline of solitude increases our patience and prepares us to engage the world. Throughout His public ministry, Jesus carved out time for isolation. Before choosing His disciples, Jesus spent the night in the desert mountains (Luke 6:12). After feeding the five thousand and hearing of John the Baptist's death, Jesus slipped away. Even the night before His crucifixion was spent alone, leaving His three closest disciples as He prayed alone (Matthew 26:36–39).

Yet it wasn't the hills or the deserted valleys that recharged the Savior's battery. To retreat for retreating's sake can't provide spiritual restoration. Rather, Jesus retreated in order to advance. He drew away for the purpose of entering into an intimate session with His Father. If we're to follow His example, we, too, must learn to back away. The Puritan writer William Gurnall wrote, "The Christian must trust in a withdrawing God."[5]

Solitude is a deliberate journey into the life-giving presence of God. While it's true that God restores the soul "beside quiet waters" (Psalm 23:2), we don't need to find an island to experience His company. Solitude is a frame of mind. It's an attitude of detachment for the purpose of attachment. Going on weekend retreats trains us to enter into the stillness of solitude, even during the frantic routines of life. With our busy schedules and pressing demands, it's unrealistic to spend gobs of time alone and unconnected. Perhaps it'd be possible if we lived two hundred years ago in the Wild Wild West, or if we grew up on the set of *Little House on the Prairie*, but those of us stuck in cities and suburbs have to be creative in our quest for solitude.

Jesus retreated in order to advance.

Transitional solitude allows us to escape the distractions of the world, even when we're right dab in the middle of them. A traffic light, an airport layover—these are perfect moments to rejuvenate the soul. An office lunch break, a drive to work—these too can be commandeered for Christ. Our transitions from point A to point B can become sacred, and you can even practice this discipline in a long checkout line at the grocery store. It's not about the location. It's about who shows up at the location.

Another way to foster transitional solitude is by leaving the church doors unlocked so people can drop in during the workweek. God's sanctuary should be a safe and welcoming place, a haven from the hassles of the world. Unlocking it only on Sundays and Wednesdays stimulates a compartmentalized Christianity within us that forgets the permeating power of God's everyday involvement.

Everyday Alps

They say the natives who live in the Himalayan Mountains have larger lungs than other people because the high altitude expands them. I've never met anyone who lived twenty thousand feet above sea level, but it makes sense. Since each breath receives less oxygen, the lung tissue improvises in order to compensate. In these conditions, they say the body even produces up to a pint more blood to increase the flow of air to the brain and muscles. Some athletes even prefer high altitude training—acclimatization, they call it.

I was speaking at a youth camp in Colorado not too long ago. The facilities were on the side of a fourteen-thousand-foot mountain, much higher than the sixteen-feet-below-sea-level city of New Orleans I was flying from. Getting off the plane in Denver (the Mile High City) was a natural rush of dizziness and disorientation. But the real spell hit me on the two-hour drive into the mountains. Sure, I thought my lungs could handle it. I was, after all, the intramural racquetball and Ping-Pong champion in college. Think again, Christian. This body was cruisin' for an altitude bruisin', and over the next few days, I felt purple and blue.

To make matters worse, I broke all the rules of hiking. I wanted to go hiking by myself to a ridge near the camp. Rule #1: Bring a friend. I didn't. Rule #2: Bring water and survival gear. Nope. To my defense, I did bring along a cell phone, but the service was spotty at best. Thinking back on it, I could have died up there, my lifeless body eaten by bears. But the words of Swedish physician Axel Munthe kept ringing in my ears: "The soul needs more space than the body."[6] So I pressed on in hopes that my soul could breathe, even though my lungs were panting.

With shallow breaths, I came to a ridge that would have made Renoir tremble with envy. Marshmallow-dipped mountains stretched above valleys of orange and yellow. God must take His vacations there. Having brought John Bunyan's *Pilgrim's Progress*, I reached into my backpack to retrieve it. But every time I looked down at the page, my eyes reverted back to the horizon. So there I sat, soaking up the altitude and the solitude with the mountain goats.

We must smuggle our Alps into our everyday lives.

I returned to that spot every day (with water and food, but still no hiking buddy). It became easier to make the hike. I didn't get as dizzy or sleepy and my breathing mellowed out. The last day of the camp I brought my Bible to the mountain to ruminate on David's words: "Be still before the Lord and wait patiently for him" (Psalm 37:7).

I suppose it's easy to wait patiently on the Lord on the side of a quiet mountain. When it comes to the activities of a twenty-first-century life, however, solitude gets tricky. But it's not impossible. In fact, it's altogether necessary. The Christian life demands inner stillness. The key to solitude is not escaping to the mountain, but rather transporting the mountain to the valley. We must smuggle our Alps into our everyday lives. We must bring them to our jobs and gyms, cram them in lockers and stuff them in luggage. No mountain is too tall, no range too wide. We can squeeze even a fourteen-thousand-footer into a carry-on suitcase—airport security won't mind at all. A daily dose of solitude increases our God-capacity. The more time we spend in the high altitude presence of Christ, the bigger our reservoir for engaging Him becomes.

Bragging Rights

We live in a country of rights—the inalienable rights of life, liberty, and the pursuit of happiness. We cherish them as those who treasure the shade of a tree they didn't plant or the security of a house they didn't build. These are our "God-given rights," sanctioned for all of us to enjoy.

But what happens when my right to happiness obstructs your right to liberty? When my right to music drowns out your right to silence? Whose right prevails? In New Testament times, there was great tension among the Jews, the Greeks, and the Romans. The Jews resented Greek polytheism, and the Greeks resented Jewish dietary guidelines and the observance of a day of rest. Both Greece and Judea hated Rome because they had both been conquered by the empire. So who does God commission to unify Greek, Jewish, and Roman Christianity? None other than Saul of Tarsus—the Jewish born, Greek-speaking Roman citizen. Paul broke down racial and cultural barriers by emphasizing unity in Christ. This is what he told the Christians living in Rome: "Do not repay anyone evil for evil. Be careful to do what is right in the eyes of everybody. If it is possible, as far as it depends on you, live at peace with everyone. Do not take revenge, my friends, but leave room for God's wrath, for it is written: 'It is mine to avenge; I will repay' says the Lord" (Romans 12:17–19).

Early Christianity had a practice for promoting unity that's still in existence today—footwashing. I've never been to a footwashing service, but according to Augustine, the practice has its perks: "For when the body is bent at a brother's feet, the feeling of such humility is either awakened in the heart itself, or is strengthened if already present."[7] In the time of Christ, a household servant removed his own garments, tied a towel around his waist, and then washed the dirt from the feet of the guests. When Jesus performed this task, it shocked the disciples. Their master, doing so menial a task! Yet Jesus said, "What I've done, you do. I'm only pointing out the obvious. A servant is not ranked above his master; an employee doesn't give orders to the employer. If you understand what I'm telling you, act like it—and live a blessed life" (John 13:14–17 MESSAGE). Practices like footwashing cultivate unity within the body of Christ and have the power to quell disputes.

Cooperation is also achieved by viewing life as a gift instead of a right. This should be easier for Christians. When it comes to our salvation, we have no rights. We can't look up at God and say, "You're obligated to save me," or "I'm entitled to heaven." It's difficult to be truly thankful for something we're owed. But grace can't be earned or inherited. It's a gift—a nonrefundable present of true freedom and liberty. So the next time some guy cuts us off in traffic and rolls down the window to show us his favorite finger, we're free to ignore it, forgive it, and go about our day.

Jesus turns our "God-given rights" upside down. Our culture values strength and stability, but Jesus said, "Happy are those who are poor in spirit." The food industry insists on being full and satisfied, but Jesus said, "Happy are those who hunger and thirst for righteousness." Talk show hosts value demeaning comebacks and demoralizing jokes, but Jesus said, "Happy are you when people insult you." Governments retaliate; Jesus forgives. We destroy our enemies; Jesus prayed for those who hurt Him. The attitudes of the Christian lie in stark contrast to the attitudes of society. So we must choose: Christ or the world?

• • •

I still go to the dollar theater. It makes for a cheap date and a good laugh. With the excellent service and the strictly enforced "no talking" rules, what's not to love? But if God can use something as loud and sticky as a movie theater to teach us patience, He can use anything—a golf course, a soccer practice, an emergency trip to the hospital. God's patience never runs out, even when ours does. But if you drop your bag of popcorn during the show, just let it go—it's gone, my friend.

"The most beautiful thing we can experience
is the mysterious."

—Albert Einstein

10 **Feng** Shui **Faith**

• • •

God's Mystery \ˈmis-t(ə)-rē\

God is an alien to us. Not the slithering kind that spews green acid and hides three rows of razor teeth. Nor the cute kind with the long E.T. neck that drinks Coke and loves everybody. God is an alien and alienated in the sense that He is distant and separate from us. He is the extraordinary *Other*.

Like a good Alfred Hitchcock film, what we can't see about God intrigues us. It moves us into the realm of curiosity where His mystery mystifies us.

Old-school theologians called this "the inscrutability of God"—the idea that He can't be completely explored or exhausted. If humans were able to squeeze God into a test tube, we ourselves would be God. Only God has a brain big enough to know Himself. If we could fully chart His greatness or view His glory, we ourselves should be worshiped. Instead, we're simple creatures—hobbits perhaps, with hairy feet and holes for homes. David was right:

"God is magnificent; he can never be praised enough. There are no boundaries to his greatness" (Psalm 145:3 MESSAGE).

Humans operate in four dimensions—height, width, depth, and time. Like a force field, these restrictions wall us in. They shackle us to this world, and even our fastest engines and state-of-the-art technologies can't free us. But nothing handcuffs God. He is bound by nothing. God surrounds Himself with infinite dimensions and robes Himself with endless realities. Having said this, I type the following pages with trembling fingers, knowing that God is too hot to handle.

> The biggest mystery . . . why a cloaked Deity would uncover Himself for a people in rebellion.

They say that in the fifth dimension you can flip a basketball inside out without puncturing it. Imagine what life is like in ten, fifteen, or fifty dimensions. Humans are shrouded from understanding the mind-boggling mysteries of God because we don't exist as He exists. Nothing in our world can be one and three at the same time. Nothing can be everywhere and in one place at once, either. But in God's reality, in God's dimension, these things do not contradict one another. They work in unison, in partnership, like the wheels and pedals of a bicycle.

God's in a league all by Himself. He has no competition; He never ties a game. In fact, when His authority came into question in the Old Testament, God spoke up: "I am God, and there is no other; I am God, and there is none like me" (Isaiah 46:9). Some have tried to mimic Him—to play God with science, power, and technology. But at the end of the day, God stands uniquely alone. No brain can decipher His frequency. No eyes can decode His wavelengths. He is distant and extraordinary, unreachable and perfectly hidden.

But He's also in plain view. The biggest mystery in the world is why a cloaked Deity would uncover Himself for a people anchored in rebellion. God gave us Himself in three ways: His Word, His Son, and His Spirit. We can also view it as His lips, His skin, and His heart. Why would God expose Himself like that? It would be one thing if God came to earth merely to analyze us. To survey or interview us. Or perhaps even to laugh at us.

But to die for us? Ouch! That's a heavy transaction, a mystery too tangled to unravel. Napoleon Bonaparte thought so. He lived an extraordinary life. What he lacked in height (he was only 5 feet 2 inches) he made up for in conquests. Over the course of his lifetime, he won forty battles, unified much of what the Roman Empire had lost, and restored the French Empire. Some even group him with those like Julius Caesar, Alexander the Great, and Charlemagne. Yet at the end of his life when faced with the life to come, the great military genius turned his thoughts from war with Europe to peace with God. While on the island of St. Helena, Napoleon said:

> I die before my time; and my dead body, too, must return to the earth to become food for worms. Behold the destiny, near at hand, of him who has been called the Great Napoleon. . . . [But] it is not so with Christ. Everything in Him astonishes me. His spirit overawes me, and His will confounds me. Between Him and whoever else in the world, there is no possible term of comparison. He is truly a being by Himself.[1]

Napoleon might have been short, but he wasn't shortsighted. He understood that there is no one like God. There is no one as beautiful or winsome. While only a handful of soldiers would have died for Napoleon during his lifetime, millions have died for the

Christ who never wielded a single weapon—and even told Peter to put away his sword (John 18:11).

Labyrinth Walking

Walking in Circles

Crop circles come in every pattern and size. Some are spiraled or star-like. Others, intricate and clustered. Some are not even circles at all—triangles, swirls, or interlacing designs. Yet all of these geometric anomalies share one thing in common—mystery. Now don't get me wrong, I'm no UFO nut, though I can quote every line from the *X-Files*. Yet the mathematical accuracies and the expansive breadth of these phenomena raise more question marks than periods.

While alien crop circles remain a mystery for most (except, of course, the guy making them with his tractor), Christians have our own circles to ponder. The discipline of labyrinth walking is a tangible way to focus our thoughts on Christ and center ourselves on God.

Labyrinths are common occurrences in God's creation. From spiderwebs to thumbprints, seashells to hurricanes, our globe swirls with labyrinths, those complicated and mysterious patterns and pathways. Archeologists believe the oldest man-made labyrinths originated in Egypt in 4500 BC.[2] Yet these circles weren't bound to this part of the world. In Peru, the Nazcan civilization (500 BC) etched spider labyrinths into the flat desert landscape, and the Hopi Indians of North America coined the "seven-path labyrinth."[3] Swedish fishermen believed labyrinths would entrap bad weather, and Greeks played tic-tac-toe-like games on them. Today Spanish bullfights reflect this tradition—a bull runs through a labyrinth of streets before opening into the center of the ring.[4]

For some cultures, labyrinths were a rite of passage, an introduction into manhood. For others, they served as art and decoration.

In the Middle Ages, Christians adopted this practice of labyrinth walking. Since pilgrimages to Jerusalem were expensive and often unrealistic, labyrinths symbolized the journey to the Holy Land and could be walked by peasants in local cathedrals. Chartres Cathedral in France, for example, was often called "The Jerusalem Road" because of the large labyrinth built into its floor. (See one version of the Chartres labyrinth on the next page.) For Christian pilgrims throughout the centuries, labyrinth walking exposed the *feng shui*—the balance, the dance—between the linear and the cyclical. For those living in medieval times, the twists and turns of life coiled with confusion and danger.

In the 1340s, the Black Death killed almost seventy-five million Europeans. Walking a planned and orderly path was a simple encouragement for those living in a world of chaos and calamity. Unlike a maze where there are dead ends, labyrinths have only one route to the center. This reminded Christians living in that time that heaven was obtainable through one path—the way of Christ. No matter how horrible the hells around them, they could be confident that God had defeated death and walked beside His suffering pilgrims.

Labyrinths can be remarkably therapeutic. Today, they're often used in therapy with children diagnosed with ADHD. Finger labyrinths, like the pattern discovered in a Neolithic tomb in Sardinia from 2500 BC, have also been shown to calm the minds and stimulate focus.[5] Hospitals have also discovered the healing benefits of labyrinth walking. Many therapy and recovery centers are equipped with circular stone and marble work integrated into the floors.

While most of us aren't within driving distance of places like the famous Chartres Cathedral, everyone can practice this discipline. If you're at the beach, sketch a pattern in the sand. If you're in the woods, outline a labyrinth with stones. If you're at home, buy a circular rug to walk around. If you're creating a backyard garden, build a labyrinth with bricks. There are even people who

Adapted from The labyrinth at Chartres Cathedral in Chartres, France.
SOURCE: www.labyrinth-enterprises.com

sell portable canvas patterns for travel.[6] For Protestants, labyrinth walking is a relatively new discipline. Of course, we practice this discipline not as a means of earning salvation but as a way to experience the God of our salvation in a new and earthy way.

So you've made or found a labyrinth. Now what? Find some music. Nonlinear chants work well. One author suggests three stages for labyrinth walking: purgation, illumination, and communion.[7] As you enter the labyrinth, don't rush. It's not about speed, it's about fellowship with God. Purge everything that distracts you from His presence. This is a great time for confession (purgation).

C. S. Lewis said, "We must lay before God what is in us, not what ought to be in us."[8] John's comfortable words encourage us that if we confess our sins to God, "he is faithful and just and will forgive us our sins and purify us from all unrighteousness" (1 John 1:9). Monks often walked the first few rings on their knees in humility and repentance before God. In the Middle Ages, cathedrals were built in the shape of crosses, and in the cases of Chartres, Amiens, and Rheims Cathedrals, the labyrinths are positioned in the cross-like layout of the church where Christ's knees would have been.[9]

Walking in circles isn't a magical tool that purifies us. . . . It's a discipline that fosters spiritual focus.

As you weave your way through the turns, fix your mind on a mystery of God—perhaps His longsuffering or eternality. Pray that God will give you insights into His nature (illumination). "You do not have, because you do not ask God" (James 4:2). God illuminates those who ask. Center your thoughts on a Bible verse or an experience you want to offer to God. Pilgrims who visited Jerusalem never arrived empty-handed. They always brought with them offerings to present to God.

After thinking, meditating, offering, praying, and asking, you will at last arrive at the center. This symbolizes the illumination—the clarity that God provides. While the center is important, it's the journey that teaches us how to arrive. You might have reached the center a dozen times while walking toward the middle of the labyrinth.

The last phase is communion. As you begin your quest out of the labyrinth, relish Christ's company. This is a time of worship and praise, a time to solidify your thoughts and feelings about Him. Praise is different than thanks. I had a seminary professor who said that when we thank God, the emphasis is still on us. But when we *praise* God, the emphasis is on God.[10]

Labyrinth walking removes us from the center of ourselves and places our thoughts on Christ. Peter reminds us that Christians are aliens in this world (1 Peter 2:11). We don't ultimately belong here, but while we are here, we must transform this place with our actions. We're pilgrims with a purpose, labyrinth-walkers who believe in Christ, our center. Walking in circles isn't a magical tool that saves or purifies us. It can't earn us grace. Rather, it's a discipline that fosters spiritual focus and helps us keep our thoughts on the Christ who is thinking about us.

Seeing the Invisible

Right now invisible forces are passing through your body. You can't see them, you can't feel them, but they're there. I don't even really understand how they work, but I do know that if I took a radio that's sensitive to their bandwidths, I could capture dozens of AM and FM frequencies. With the right equipment I could hear everything from National Public Radio to *The Rick and Bubba Show*.[11]

In Luke 8, Jesus asks His disciples a very important question: "Where is your faith?" (v. 25). At the beginning of Luke 8, the disciples had gallons of faith. They had listened to Jesus' sermon about the sower and believed that God had planted them in Galilee for a reason. They heard Him describe the lamp on the stand and dared to be firecrackers against the midnight backdrop. Even when they stepped into the boat, their faith was thoroughly intact.

But then came the spinning labyrinth of life. A storm appeared in the sky and the bowels of the lake churned with swirling currents. Waves beleaguered their first-century wooden vessel and soon buoyancy became a problem. Yet all the while Jesus was beneath the bow, catching up on some sleep. The God whose eye was "on the sparrow" was getting some peaceful shut-eye. And the disciples were reduced to skeptics.

When Jesus woke up from His sleep, He saw the panic in their eyes. He saw their lack of faith and vision. Surely they knew that it wasn't their times to die. It wasn't *His* time to die, either. The Old Testament prophecies would have been wasted if the Messiah drowned in a fishing accident. Jesus came to die on a cross, not in a canoe. That's why in the midst of the storm, Jesus could get some REM sleep. A little water couldn't wash away the flood of God's love for His people.

Yet there would be no one to hush the Golgotha tempest. Jesus would be all alone in that boat, all alone to face the fury of sin and abandonment. But for the moment, Jesus put the Sea of Galilee on an ironing board and straightened it out.

We live in an age of visual stimulation, an age of plasma screens and high-definition channels. We want life as clear and crisp as possible. But there's something beautiful, something biblical, about focusing on the invisible. There's something satisfying about trusting God with our eyes closed. Jesus told Thomas, "Blessed are those who have not seen and yet believe" (John 20:29).

Paul reminds us to "fix our eyes not on what is seen, but on what is unseen" (2 Corinthians 4:18). With modern telescopes, we can see two hundred and fifty planets outside our solar system,[12] including those like HD189733B, a Jupiter-like planet that has methane gas in its atmosphere.[13] Yet as technologically advanced as we are, even our smartest scientists are reduced to children pointing up at a mysterious sky. To believe in anything requires faith in something. And we can persevere through life as Moses, who saw "him who was invisible" (Hebrews 11:27). Faith is like a Magic Eye puzzle—we look through the physical to see the spiritual. We look through the immediate to see the eternal. And when we cast our eyes on God, worlds of images appear as if from nowhere.

On Paw Paw's Living Room Floor

They called him Brother Williams and he was a prince of a man. He was a preacher and evangelist, a musician and inventor. I only have a handful of memories of my great-grandfather—he died when I was four. But I remember that he raised goats in his backyard and put them to work like Oompa Loompas. He built a four-hundred- yard zip line from his house to the barbershop where he worked, and he also rigged a contraption so that when he woke up in the morning, all he had to do to turn on the radio was wiggle his little toe. He was one of the first people in Tennessee to record his voice into a machine and then use it as background harmony when he sang. He called it "George, George, and the Lord." He was a character. Once he even got so mad at a misbehaving horse that he flat out punched it in the face. They say the horse hit the ground.

The more we "hang with the Holy," the holier we become.

I remember sitting on the floor of Paw Paw's living room, experimenting with a set of round, black magnets. Magnetism was strange magic for a preschooler—an alien technology. I couldn't quite wrap my mind around it. For unknown reasons, the little objects resisted one another. No matter how hard I pushed them together, they repelled with stubborn resistance. Yet when I flipped them around, they bonded so forcefully that I could barely pry them apart.

We may never fully understand how God invisibly draws us to Himself, but one thing is for sure: the closer we get to God, the stronger our love for Him grows. The more we "hang with the Holy," the holier we become. While there is a repelling side of

God—a magnetic south—no one who seeks salvation has ever seen it. Spiritual disciplines like labyrinth walking, prayer, meditation, and fasting hold us in tight proximity to Christ. We might not see Him with our eyes or touch Him with our hands, but He's near. He's close enough to whisper our names. Jesus said, "Whoever humbles himself like this child, is the greatest in the Kingdom of heaven" (Matthew 18:4 NASB).

God doesn't want us to be childish; He wants us to child*like*. To have a faith that walks hand in hand with God even though we can't see what's around the corner. To sit at His feet and listen to His stories, for within His words lie the answers to life's deepest mysteries. Sometimes we can be so busy with good things, even great things, that we forget the best thing: to be with God and enjoy His company.

Before his death in 1996, Henri Nouwen shared a story about a trapeze artist named Rodleigh who became his friend. Nouwen was mesmerized by how the flyer released the trapeze, soared through the air, and then was caught by the other trapeze artist. He had to ask how the stunt was executed.

"As a flyer," Rodleigh said, "I must have complete trust in my catcher. The public might think that I am the great star of the trapeze, but the real star is Joe, my catcher. He has to be there for me with split-second precision and grab me out of the air as I come to him in the long jump. . . . The secret is that the flyer does nothing and the catcher does everything."

"Nothing?" Nouwen replied.

"Nothing. The worst thing the flyer can do is try to catch the catcher. . . . If I grab Joe's wrists, I might break them, or he might break mine, and that would be the end of both of us. A flyer must fly, and a catcher must catch, and the flyer must trust, with outstretched arms, that the catcher will be there for him."[14]

God never drops His catch. In this circus of life, we release the trapeze and soar through the day—flying down highways, flailing from one activity to the next. We spin and somersault from here to there while life and death hang in the balance. One slipup, one car accident, and that would be "all she wrote." Yet we can trust the Catcher. Christ never loses what He wins. Like a magnet, grace comes for us, screeching toward us with hands outstretched. God will never let us fall; He has invested too much in our development. God is alien to us, but He has come down to our planet. The celestial has swung to the terrestrial. And Christians are caught by the Catcher.

• • •

They say when you lose one sense you gain another. When sight is lost, sound is amplified. When sound is lost, touch is magnified. When all is dark and dumb in the world, we must embrace the blindness to see Christ; we must embrace the deafness to hear Him. And by expanding our faith to fit an expansive God, we can experience His mysteries afresh.

"Cheese . . . milk's leap toward immortality."

—Clifton Fadiman

11

G-Force

• • •

God's Eternality \ē-tər-nal-i-tē\

Everything that begins must come to an end—classes, books, weekends, spring break. We are a people who understand the life and death, the A and Z of things. After three years of faithful repairs, even my Apple Protection Plan refuses to cover a laptop facing digital decay.

But God has no beginning. He is the *Forever Then*, the *Eternal Now*, and the *Endless Will Be*. He is the Distant Past who spills into the Immediate Present, the Ancient History involved in the Current Events. In God's time zone, clocks drip into puddles at His throne.

Humans can't escape time, but we can define it. The Greeks had two words for time, *chronos* and *kairos*. *Chronos* is horizontal time, one minute after the next. It's the time that appears in the corner of a video camera. *Kairos*, on the other hand, is momentary time. It's the snapshot in the photo album, the memory that stands out. Both *chronos* and *kairos* help us categorize our time, but even they can't free us from it. Time is a slippery substance, a greasy creature. The moment you hold it in your hand, it vanishes through your fingers. How do you even define the present? Is it the morphing of past to future? Is it the evolution of "was" to "is"? How long does that take? A second? A millisecond? A nanosecond?

Time machines have long been the subject of movies and science fiction novels. Time travel excites us. It's incredible to think that we could move through time like one moves through rooms or hallways. A mistake you want to fix? Hop in the time machine! A girlfriend you should have dumped? Start the ignition! Yet the closest we come to time travel is our memories. We can't change the past, but we can revisit it. We can also project ourselves into the future by imagining what we'll be doing a year or decade from now. But our fundamental problem is that we are truly plastered to the present.

God is outside of time, yet He can enter and control it whenever He wishes.

But not God. "You're from eternity, aren't you?" Habakkuk asked (Habakkuk 1:12). The author of Hebrews answers: "Jesus doesn't change—yesterday, today, tomorrow, he's always totally himself" (Hebrews 13:8). Time is a suggestion for God, not a rule. Before approaching Pharaoh with the "Let my people go" bit, Moses needed to know God's name in case the Israelites asked. This is what God said: "I-AM-WHO-I-AM. Tell the people of Israel, 'I-AM sent me to you'" (Exodus 3:14). When Jesus was on earth, He also claimed this title. He told the Jews, "Believe me, I am who I am long before Abraham was anything" (John 8:57–59). (All Scripture in this paragraph is from *The Message*.)

Albert Einstein theorized that if an object traveled as fast as the speed of light (seven hundred million miles per hour), for that object, time would stand still. If it went faster than that, time would reverse. God not only bathes in light, He is Light. "In him there is no darkness" (1 John 1:5). Space and time have no hold on God. Friction and wind resistance can't slow Him down. Speedometers and odometers can't measure His movement. God is outside of time, yet He can enter and control it whenever He wishes. Like Superman spinning around the world to bring Lois Lane back from the dead, Jesus reversed the effects of aging and death on His friend Lazarus (John 11:44). But for Ananias and Sapphira who stole from God, He sped them up and they fell over dead (Acts 5). Once, God even paralyzed the universe so Joshua could spend an extra day fighting on the battlefield (Joshua 10).

After Jesus rose from the dead, the disciples were gathered in a room. The door was locked, and suddenly Jesus appeared before them (John 20:26). They thought He was a ghost or spirit because how can a man materialize from thin air? Jesus told them ghosts can't be touched, and He invited Thomas to touch His side.

Jesus could appear, and He could also disappear. Like the time the two men from the road to Emmaus invited Him over for dinner. After breaking bread, Jesus immediately vanished from their sight (Luke 24:31). The two men rushed to find the eleven disciples to tell them what had happened, and "while they were still talking" Jesus appeared in their presence (Luke 24:36). We don't know how Jesus teleported so quickly, but one thing's certain: God travels at the speed of God. David wrote:

> Where can I go from your Spirit?
> Where can I flee from your presence?
> If I go up to the heavens, you are there.
> If I rise on the wings of the dawn,
> if I settle on the far side of the sea,
> even when your hand will guide me, your right hand will hold me fast. (Psalm 139:7–10)

Time and location cannot limit God, and His Spirit freely moves throughout the world.

Redout

During the Vietnam War, fighter jets like the F-4 Phantom and the F-105 Thunderchief were built as "stable aircrafts." When a pilot pulled back on the stick, it was nearly impossible for the Gs exerted on the wings to damage the aircraft (a "G" is a multiple of the earth's gravity. At nine Gs, a 200-pound pilot weighs 1,800 pounds). Thanks to the evolution of fighter jet technology, we can now construct "unstable" aircrafts like the F-16 Fighting Falcon and the F/A-18 Hornet that can go faster. The problem is they can literally tear themselves to pieces by taking too sharp a turn.

Modern pilots must wear G-suits and also be in outstanding shape to withstand the demands these new aircrafts place on the human body. If a pilot pulls up too quickly, the blood sinks out of his brain and pools in the lower regions of the body. Unless the pilot is physically prepared for the turn, he blacks out. If, on the other hand, a pilot pushes the aircraft down too quickly, the blood rushes to his head and redout occurs.

America is experiencing a G-force blackout. We're losing our spiritual consciousness. The higher we climb, the less God's presence impresses us. The taller we stand, the shorter our tolerance of Him grows. Just look around. We can do just fine without Him. It's easy to run our churches without God. All we need is a dedicated planning committee, a few building projects, and a spiritual retreat sprinkled here and there. Yet with Mary Magdalene we confess, "They have taken my Lord away . . . and I don't know where they have put him" (John 20:13). God has a sobering message for America: How high can I lift you before I lose you?[1]

The blood of Christ is pooling in the southern hemisphere. It's draining from earth's forehead to places like South America, India, and Asia where revivals and awakenings are exploding. Take Africa—a continent familiar with shepherds, famine, idolatry, and animal sacrifice. The Bible frequently speaks to them in a way it doesn't speak to us.[2] I love the Baptist hymn that asks, "Are you washed in the blood of the lamb?"[3] But I've never been washed in the blood of an animal (I did drown a hamster once, but let's not get into that). To tell someone who regularly sacrifices sheep in Zimbabwe that Jesus Christ is the Lamb that was slain—well, now you're speaking their language. The gospel instantly resonates. For the family who prays to carved wooden figures in Ethiopia, Samuel's words take on fresh meaning: "Do not turn away after useless idols. They can do you no good, nor can they rescue you, because they are useless" (1 Samuel 12:21). For the Tuareg tribes living in the Sahara desert, God's ability to "keep them alive in famine" (Psalm 33:19) goes a long way.

In the midst of our American blackout—our fainting faith—there are pockets of redouts. New generations of Christians are thinking crimson thoughts. We're trying to live Christ-centered lives in a human-centered world. Against the flow of postmodernity, we're insisting on God's truth anchored in God's Word. God has become our daily bread and butter, and we're starving for more.

Practicing God's Presence

Feeling His Pleasure

Brother Lawrence was a simple monk. His real name was Nicholas Herman, but when he joined a monastery, he gave up his name and all his possessions. Brother Lawrence didn't own much or know a lot. He wasn't much to look at and probably couldn't tell a decent joke. His feet were crippled and he developed a reputation for being a rather clumsy guy. He spent an entire year dreading his turn to buy groceries in the marketplace for his monastery. Yet Brother Lawrence did one thing and one thing very well.

The dishes. No one could scrub them better. Forks feared him, bowls revered him. To the astonishment of his friends, Brother Lawrence felt God's presence more in the kitchen than the cathedral.[4] "Lord of all pots and pans and things," he prayed, "make me a saint by getting meals and washing up the plates!"[5] No matter how simple the job, Brother Lawrence found God's company in it. "We can do little things for God; I turn the cake that is frying on the pan for love of Him."[6] Even taking out the trash became a God-infused moment for him.

Wherever we are, whatever we're doing, we can live in God's presence.

Scottish runner Eric Liddell said, "God made me fast, and when I run I feel His pleasure."[7] Where do you feel God's pleasure? Placing an IV in a patient's arm? Unscrewing an oil filter? Studying about endoplasmic reticulum for a cell biology exam? Wherever we are, whatever we're doing, we can live in God's presence. When we're painting a picture, practicing a violin, or playing a game of putt-putt, we can develop a heightened awareness of God's interaction in our lives.

Before the days of global positioning satellites and pinpoint precision maps, marine explorers used a tool called a sextant to locate their position on the water. Invented in 1731, sextants incorporated a dual mirror system that allowed the captain to see both the sun and the horizon. The measurement between these two angles determined a ship's latitude. Christopher Columbus used an astrolabe (the precursor of the sextant) to locate the North Star on his quest for India, as did Magellan on his world travels. Modern sextants are accurate enough to locate a position within a few hundred feet.

Practicing God's presence is a tool every pilgrim can use. It helps us understand where we are and where we need to go.

It points us upward and outward to determine our inward. It is a mixture of all the disciplines and, like a coda, it sends us back to the beginning to practice them all and live in constant awareness of God. Practicing God's presence reminds us to focus not on the disciplines themselves, but rather on the God to whom the disciplines point. You and I are not responsible for the future or the past. God only holds us accountable for the present, for this moment—right now, this second, this word, this syllable—is an opportunity to be faithful and obedient to Christ.

To be a Christian is to lift our eyes to God and extend our arms to others. Only then can we truly know ourselves. After looking up at God, Job said, "How great God is beyond our understanding!" (Job 36:26). After lowering his chin, Job turned to his three friends and saved their lives by praying for their pardon (Job 42:7–9). James summarized: "Faith [upward] without deeds [outward] is useless" (James 2:20).

The discipline of God's presence trumps all disciplines. It's the ultimate aim of solitude, silence, hospitality, meditation, and the others. To incorporate God's presence in life's routine is the highest goal of the Christian. Nothing eclipses this. To think of Christ in the monotonous times, to yearn and burn for Him in the boring times—these become our tenderest moments, our self-defining *kairos*. When we practice His presence we become aware of His awareness, and we can savor the Savior.

That's where our brokenness meets His beauty, and the sum of our pain meets the power of His purpose. That's true worship—when the God who exists in the forever enters our now. To be in that spot, to live in this way, is to massage the soul with heavenly jets. And to sink your teeth into that kind of Christianity can cause an addictive frenzy. Knowing God intimately can become a habit-forming endeavor. To be in the presence of God is the greatest undertaking of the human spirit. It's our ultimate destination, our big safari. And to be there is to be home.

A Rule for the Road

Christianity is not a Slip 'N Slide. Jonathan Edwards said, "The way to heaven is ascending; we must be content to travel uphill."[8] Ours is a pilgrimage of angles, a journey of ups and downs, hells and heavens. But we don't travel without a God or a guide.

Throughout the history of Christianity, many pilgrims have benefited from writing and following a Rule of Life—a set of practices that directed their steps. The Rule of Saint Benedict and the Rule of Saint Francis are widely practiced by Christians around the world. But you don't have to live in a monastery or convent to adhere to a rule. Martin Luther King Jr. wrote a rule for those participating in the nonviolent protests in Birmingham, Alabama. Some of his rules were:

> Meditate daily on the teachings and life of Jesus.
> Walk and talk in the manner of love, for God is love.
> Seek justice and reconciliation, not victory.
> Observe with both friend and foe the ordinary rules of courtesy.
> Seek to perform regular service for others and the world.
> Strive to be in good spiritual and bodily health.[9]

Humans resist rules. We make them only to bend or break them. As kids we hate rules like brushing our teeth or waiting an hour after lunch to swim in the deep end. The word itself generates great opposition in us—*rule* comes from the Latin *regula*, meaning "straight stick." It automatically puts us on the defensive. When I think of rules or rulers, I think about some movie where the angry nun goes berserk on her disobedient student.

The monks who lived with Saint Benedict in Italy hated his rules so much that they tried to poison him. It's no surprise that

Benedict included this rule in his Rule: "Let the monks sleep clothed and girded with belts or cords—but not with their knives at their sides, lest they cut themselves in their sleep."[10] The rules of Saint Clare were even stricter. She slept on a bundle of twigs with a log for a pillow and wore a dress made of pigskin with the bristles on the inside.[11]

Rules, whether strict or lax, should always point us to Christ. They should enable us to train for godliness. Any professional understands this. A med student training to be a surgeon is no stranger to the rigor of rules—studying all night for tests, living off three hours of sleep during residency. A concert clarinetist understands the rules necessary for excelling at the instrument. Olympic snowboarders structure their entire lives around rules that keep them on the slopes, come frost or come freeze. Lawyers, zoologists, professors, and actors are masters of rules, disciplining themselves to be good at their jobs. James Rohn said, "We must all suffer one of two things: the pain of discipline or the pain of regret or disappointment."[12]

So why not Christians? Faith isn't just a hobby; it's an all-consuming existence. For those who take their Christianity seriously, a rule of life can be a valuable sextant. So how do you get started? Make a list of twenty or more goals that you want to work toward in your spiritual life. Let's say one goal is "I want to become a person who edifies everyone around me with my words." Seek God's guidance as to which spiritual disciplines or practices will best enable you to develop an encouraging countenance. Or maybe your goal is to spend one day a month in complete silence, just listening to others and learning how to really hear people.

This is your set of rules, tailored to your needs and desires. Maybe you need to get a better grasp of the Bible. Spend an entire year practicing the discipline of Scripture memorization. Maybe you need healing or direction in a specific area of your life, or clarity for a future decision. Maybe you need to be more well rounded.

Try reading a book from your polar opposite (for me that would be *Fundamentals of Differential Equations* by Kent Nagle).

In the hands of a dedicated Christian, a Rule of Life can be a powerful navigational instrument. It can aid us in practicing the presence of God. We should not broadcast our rules to the world, but know that the world is watching to see if God has really made a difference in our lives.

Life was never meant to be flown on autopilot. There are too many adventures to take, too many discoveries to make. It's easy to cruise at forty thousand feet above the earth without the rush of finding your own path. But life's too short to be lived in the clouds. There's a new breed of Christian in this country—an alien breed, a pilgrim people with wings to spread and Gs to pull. We're ready to risk, to move from the safe to the scary. To engage the deep mysteries beneath us. Martyn Lloyd-Jones said, "You can be so interested in great theological and intellectual and philosophical problems that you tend to forget that you are going to die."[13] That's why Jonathan Edwards included this in his rule of life: "Resolved to live with all my might, while I do live."[14]

• • •

One of my favorite memories is walking through a foggy Scottish cemetery with my dad. I was just a kid, but it was one of those moments you never really forget—a timeless moment that's seared on the skull. I remember looking at the chiseled words on the gravestones, words like, "Here lies Finola, asleep in the Lord," and "Here lies Willie, a friend of God." As I walked through the overgrown cemetery, I'll never forget the words I saw on one particular stone. The name had been smoothed beyond recognition but I could make out the epitaph:

AS YOU ARE

I WAS.

AS I AM

YOU WILL BECOME.

On our gravestones there will be two dates: the date of our births and the date of our deaths. We can't necessarily control those two numbers, but we can control the dash in between them. What will you do with your dash? Freeze it for later? Splurge it on weekends? Dashes can rust if we neglect them. But God is in the dash-redeeming business. He bleaches them with grace and dips them in glory. He gives us fresh starts and new beginnings.

So hit the throttle! Blast away. Twist your dash into a life of mach-three thrill. Fly the skies fast enough to make a pterodactyl jealous. God will soar beside you, above you, and around you. And when it's time to land—when it's time for home—Christ will clear the runway and lead you to your hangar up in heaven.

"You are the salt of the earth."

—Jesus (Matthew 5:13)

Epilogue
(NaCl)

• • •

Sodium Chloride \sō-dē-əm\ \klôr-īd\

"Pants down!"

I looked at her with fearful eyes. "I'm actually going to leave them on, thanks."

"Pants down now!" she said in her limited English.

She was serious and I was scared. I waited for her to leave the room, but she wouldn't budge an inch. Reluctantly, I dropped my drawers and prepared for the most awkward moment of my life. This was our first time in the Holy Land, so my wife and I had to try the infamous Dead Sea mud wrap. They say a salt and seaweed treatment is great for the body—a real energizer. Lying sunny-side up on a plastic-covered table, I had my doubts.

"You be still," she said, caking me in molten mud.

Like I had a choice. I was a muddy mummy, a human burrito. This was far from the Brookstone massagers I knew back home. And to make matters worse I could only move my fingers. That is, until the mud began to dry.

After our eye-opening spa treatment, my wife and I jumped into the Dead Sea. With a salt concentration of 30 percent (most oceans are around 3 percent), nothing sinks to the bottom. Having cut myself shaving, I floated in agonizing awkwardness. The weightlessness was foreign to me—like an astronaut experiencing his first planetary orbit. But soon my flailing ceased, my neck relaxed, and I embraced the mysterious cushion beneath me.

God is a mystery too dense to penetrate. The best we can do is lean back and marvel at His majesty. When we engage Him, when we swim and soak in His truth, we discover that He's able to support our weight. He heals us and doesn't let us sink. Joe Church, a missionary to Africa, said, "Revival is not when the roof blows off, but when the bottom falls out."[1] The bottom is falling out beneath ordinary people across America—college students, artists, nurses, waiters, writers, singers, computer programmers. In offices everywhere, Christ is pulling the fire alarm of our hearts and ushering us to worship. It's time to trade a casual faith for a crucial one, to practice disciplines that strip us before the God who clothes us. Our old platforms are crashing away. Our old paradigms are falling apart. We're splashing into the invisible arms of the Almighty. And feeling is permeating the numb limbs of Christ—it's time to tingle!

This book has been my exploration of God, my Jesus mud-wrap. Yet it's far from complete. The deeper I dig into God's attributes, the shallower I find myself. The harder I shovel, the thicker the ground. How can anyone describe the Indescribable? How can mortal lips pronounce the Unpronounceable? Perhaps if our vocal chords had a thousand octaves or our language, a million syllables. But to perfectly articulate the glory of God requires tongues we don't have, words we can't say, and alphabets we don't know. Books about God are never truly finished, only orphaned. And now I abandon this one in hopes that you'll pick up where I left off.

Life is messy. It's covered in plaque and problems. We want a world that's white, but instead it's stained. But in the middle of our mess, God puts a fresh taste in our mouths. He seasons us with salt. He teaches us that faith must fall from our lips to our hearts. Only then can it circulate in our bloodstream and change every part of us. We can hope in a hope like that.

God's narrative never ends, yet He has invested Himself in our short stories. "Like an open book, you watched me grow from conception to birth; all the stages of my life were spread out before you" (Psalm 139:15 MESSAGE). God could have created us as caricatures, but instead He spared no expense in our sophisticated sagas. Each sinew is complex. Each synapse, delicate.

Humans are God's antonyms—born in opposition to the Author. But our plots can thicken. Our characters can develop. God writes us, rewrites us, and then copyrights us in Christ. And that's why we can live each chapter as though it might be our last. God has fused His story to ours and has given us an awesome ending—a happily ever after ending.

So keep writing. Keep living. Keep traveling from one page to the next. You might get paper cuts here and there, but who knows where your journey will lead? Who knows how your epic will end? It might just take you to a sea of salt, a place where all things float in perfect mystery—a place called *Godology*.

the ~~end~~

\be-ˈgi-niŋ\

Notes

Introduction: Rakes for Shovels

1. A. W. Tozer, *The Knowledge of the Holy* (New York: Harper & Row, 1961), 9.
2. As Mr. Beaver tells Lucy in *The Lion, the Witch, and the Wardrobe*, Aslan the almighty lion is not safe, "but he is good. He's the King"; C. S. Lewis, *The Lion, the Witch, and the Wardrobe* (1950; repr., New York: HarperCollins, 2005), 81.

Chapter 1: Mardi Gras and Icicles

1. As I heard Rhyme Putnam, a seminary doctoral student, describe God in May 2008 during a Sunday school class at Calvary Baptist Church in Algiers, Louisiana.
2. *Trinity* is a term first used by Theophilus of Antioch (AD 168–181/8) and Tertullian (c.AD 207).
3. St. Augustine expounds on this in *De trinitate* XV. xxii. 42.
4. I first heard this analogy in spring 2008, during a chapel sermon by Tony Merida, then dean of chapel and assistant professor of preaching, New Orleans Baptist Seminary (now senior pastor of First Baptist Church, Kenner, Louisiana).
5. The Jesus Prayer. This is an ancient prayer, uttered by millions of Christians for a thousand years.
6. This is from a portion of "St. Patrick's Breastplate," a prayer that originated in Ireland either in the fifth or eighth century. It is also called "The Deer's Cry" or "The Lorica," and is a part of the *liber Hymnorum*, a collection of hymns.
7. Francis A. Schaeffer, *The Mark of the Christian* (1970; repr. Downers Grove, Ill.: InterVarsity, 2007), 22.
8. National Education Association of the United States, *Addresses and Proceedings-National Education Association of the United States, 1873* (Ann Arbor, Mich.: Univ. of Michigan, 2007), 31.
9. Charles Spurgeon, *Spurgeon Gold*, comp. Ray Comfort (Jacksonville, Fla.: Bridge-Logos, 2005), 15.
10. John Russell, the Philip Jenkins Lectures, Beeson Divinity School, Birmingham, Alabama, March 11, 2008.
11. Arnold A. Dallimore, *George Whitefield* (Wheaton, Ill.: Crossway, 1990), 67.
12. This is an adaptation of Debbie Blue's phrase, "Glory doesn't shine, it bleeds," in *Sensual Orthodoxy* (St. Paul, Minn.: Cathedral Hill, 2003), 127.

Chapter 2: Jesus Ninja

1. The first indoor toilet was created by Isaac Rogers and installed in the Tremont Hotel in Boston in 1829. http://www.theplumber.com/usa.html
2. Albert Einstein, quoted in Alice Calaprice and Trevor Lipscombe, *Albert Einstein* (Westport, Conn.: Greenwood Press, 2005), 92.
3. Often said by Dr. Robert Smith, Jr., Associate Professor of Divinity, Beeson Divinity School, Birmingham, Alabama.
4. Karl Barth, *Church Dogmatics* (Edinburgh, Scotland: T & T Clark, 1961), 49.
5. Charles Spurgeon, quoted in "Good Question: Text Criticism and Inerrancy" by J. I. Packer in *Christianity Today*, October 7, 2002.

6. N. Keijzer, *Military Obedience* (New York: Springer, 1978), 72.
7. William Smith, *Dictionary of Greek and Roman Antiquities* (London: John Murray, 1891), 688.
8. J. B. Phillips, *Your God Is Too Small* (New York: Touchstone, 2004), 7.

Chapter 3: Sunsets and Dinosaurs

1. Charles Spurgeon, *Morning and Evening* (1994; repr., Ross-shire, Scotland: Christian Focus, 2000), March 21 Evening.
2. Tom Mueller, "Biomimetics: Design by Nature," *National Geographic*, April 2008, 82.
3. Ibid.
4. Bill Bryson, *A Short History of Nearly Everything* (New York: Broadway, 2004), 134.
5. A. W. Tozer, *Whatever Happened to Worship?* ed. Gerald B. Smith, (Camp Hill, Penn.: Christian Publications, 1985), 44.
6. Jonathan Edwards, quoted in Maud Van Buren, *Quotations for Special Occasions* (New York: Van Doren, 2007), 177.
7. John Calvin, quoted in Rich Wagner, *The Myth of Happiness* (Grand Rapids: Zondervan, 2007), 38.
8. Robert Browning, *The Complete Poetic and Dramatic Works of Robert Browning* (Cambridge, England: Houghton Mifflin, 1895), 36.
9. Carl Sagan, quoted in Thomas Wilson, *Innovative Reward Systems for the Changing Workplace*, 2nd ed. (Columbus, Ohio: McGraw-Hill, 2002), 55.
10. At the Church of Fools, found at http://www.churchoffools.com, Internet guests can enter a two dimensional or three dimensional sanctuary, where visitors can "choose a cartoon character, enter the church, walk around, sit in a pew, explore the sanctuary and crypt, key in some prayers, and even ring the church bells." At St. Pixels, http://www.stpixels.com/view_releases.cgi, visitors can "meet others, talk about serious and not-so-serious stuff, discuss what you do and don't believe, go to regular services, and join a pioneering worldwide community."
11. Mark Galli, *Beyond Smells & Bells: The Wonder and Power of Christian Liturgy* (Brewster, Mass.: Paraclete, 2008), 26.
12. Maurice Lévy, Jean Liopoulos Raymond Gastmans, and Jean-Marc Gérard, eds., *Masses of Fundamental Particles Cargèse 1996: Nato Science Series* B, 237 (n.p.: Springer, 1997), at http://amapedia.amazon.com/view/Masses+of+Fundamental+Particles:+Cargèse+1996+(NATO+Science+Series:+B:)/asin=030645694X

Chapter 4: Showing Some Skin

1. Lyric from "God Speaking"; written by Ronnie Freeman and sung by *American Idol* finalist Mandisa Hundley in 2006 (season five).
2. Charles Spurgeon, *Sermons of Rev. C. H. Spurgeon of London* (New York: Robert Carter & Brothers, 1883), 869.
3. *The Oprah Winfrey Show*, Show #W265, air date September 18, 1987, official transcript.
4. Dan Brown, *The Da Vinci Code* (New York: Anchor, 2006), 244.
5. The Barna Group, "Americans Draw Theological Beliefs from Diverse Points of View," October 8, 2002; http://www.barna.org/FlexPage.aspx?Page=BarnaUpdate&BarnaUpdateID=122

6. Adapted from the Breastplate of Laidcenn, Calvin Miller, *The Path of Celtic Prayer* (Downers Grove, Ill.: InterVarsity, 2007), 126.
7. Timothy George, during a conversation with the author at Beeson Divinity School, Birmingham, Alabama.
8. Scot Bessenecker, quoted in "The New Monasticism" by Rob Moll, *Christianity Today*, September 2005.
9. Shane Claiborne, *The Irresistible Revolution: Living as an Ordinary Radical* (Grand Rapids: Zondervan, 2006), 117.
10. Richard Wurmbrand, *100 Prison Meditations: Cries of Truth from Behind the Iron Curtain* (Bartlesville, Okla.: Bridge-Logos, 1984), 15.
11. Mother Teresa, *No Greater Love* (New York: New World Library, 2002), 94.
12. Richard Wurmbrand, *100 Prison Meditations: Cries of Truth from Behind the Iron Curtain* (Bartlesville, Okla.: Voice of the Martyrs, 2004), 14.
13. You can subscribe to Voice of the Martyrs at: www.persecution.com and Bibles Unbound at: www.www.biblesunbound.com/qry/mc_home.taf

Chapter 5: Chocolate for the Soul

1. Tim Riter, *Not a Safe God* (Nashville: B&H Publishing, 2006), 9.
2. Paul Tawrell, *Camping & Wilderness Survival* (n.p.: Tawrell, 2006), 675.
3. See Exod. 13:21; 19:9; 24:15; 33:9; Num. 9:15; 16:42; 1 Kings 8:10; Ps. 97:2; 99:7; Isa. 6:4; 30:27; Ezek. 1:28; Matt. 17:5; Mark 13:26; Luke 9:34; Acts 1:9; 1 Thess. 4:17; Rev. 1:7; 10:1; 14:14.
4. Plato, quoted in John Robbins and Peter Kahle, *The Power of Spirituality in Therapy* (New York: Routledge: 2004), 25.
5. Arthur W. Knapp, *Cocoa and Chocolate* (n.c.: Crawford Press, 2007), 7.
6. Andrew Dalby, *Dangerous Tastes* (Berkeley, Calif.: Univ. of California Press, 2002), 145.
7. *Painting a New World: Mexican Art and Life, 1521–1821* (Denver: Denver Art Museum, 2004), 40.
8. Gardner C. Taylor, speaking at the E. K. Bailey International Conference, Dallas, July 2003, says we will be so holy that when we stand next to Christ, someone may ask, "Now which of you is Jesus?"
9. John Owen, *Pneumatologia* 3:5, in *The Works of John Owen DD*, vol. 3, ed. W. H. Gold (1850–55; repr., London and Edinburgh: Johnstone and Hunger, 1965–68), 325.
10. J. C. Ryle, *Holiness*, 3rd ed. (London: William Hunt & Co., 1887), 29.
11. Richard J. Foster and Emilie Griffin, *Spiritual Classics: Selected Readings for Individuals and Groups on the Twelve Spiritual Disciplines* (New York: HarperOne, 2000), xiii.
12. Knapp, *Cocoa and Chocolate*, 11.
13. George Rapitis, *The Lighter Side of Dark Chocolate* (Bloomington, Ind.: AuthorHouse, 2007), 12.
14. Andrea Peirce, *The American Pharmaceutical Association Practical Guide to Natural Medicines* (New York: William Morrow, 1999), 186.
15. Henri Nouwen, quoted in Deirdre LaNoue, *The Spiritual Legacy of Henri Nouwen* (Continuum International Publishing Group, 2000), 79.
16. John Michael Talbot, *The Fire of God* (Berryville, Ark.: Troubadour for the Lord, 1993), 90.

17. J. I. Packer, selected and introduced by Alister McGrath, *The J. I. Packer Collection* (Downers Drove, Ill.: InterVarsity, 1999), 75.
18. Marcus Tullius Cicero, as quoted in Hannah More, *The Works of Hannah More* (New York: Harper & Brothers Publishers, 1852), 555.
19. Hank Rubin, *The Kitchen Answer Book* (Herndon, Va.: Capital Books, 2002), 61.
20. The surprising report, entitled "Hidden Slaves: Forced Labor in the United States," summarizes conditions found by University of California Berkeley's Human Rights Center in 2004. See Janet Gilmore, "Modern Slavery Thriving in the US," UC Berkeley News, 23 September, 2004. http://berkeley.edu/news/media/releases/2004/09/23_16691.shtml
21. Rima Salah, "Child Trafficking in West and Central Africa"; Paper presented at the Pan African Conference on Human Trafficking, at the University of Newcastle, February 2001.
22. Gerard Reed, *C. S. Lewis and the Bright Shadow of Holiness* (Kansas City: Beacon Hill, 1999),19.

Chapter 6: Rhapsody in Red

1. Timothy and Denise George, *Dear Unborn Child* (Nashville: Broadman, 1984), 73.
2. John Piper, *God Is the Gospel* (Wheaton, Ill.: Crossway, 2005), 13.
3. Coach Castille played college football for the Alabama Crimson Tide under legendary coach Bear Bryant and six seasons in the National Football League (1983–88) before teaching physical education and Bible classes at Briarwood Christian High School (1995–2002). Currently, he is the chaplain of the University of Alabama football team. See www.jeremiahcastille.com
4. Richard J. Foster, *Celebration of Discipline* (San Francisco: HarperSanFrancisco, 1998), 55.
5. Tertullian, quoted in John Kaye, *The Ecclesiastical History of the Second and Third Centuries: Illustrated from the Writings of Tertullian* (Eugene, Oreg.: Wipf and Stock, 2006), 428.

Chapter 7: Jealous Is My Name

1. Jim Carrey, www.wikiquote.org/wiki/Jim_Carrey
2. John Michael Talbot, *The Fire of God* (Berryville, Ark.: Troubadour for the Lord, 1993), 119.
3. Charles Q. Chol, "Naked Mole Rats Can't Feel Burning Pain," by Fox News, January 30, 2008, www.foxnews.com/story/0,2933,326355,00.html#
4. Oswald Chambers, quoted in Martin H. Manser, ed., *The Westminster Collection of Christian Quotations* (Louisville, Ky.: Westminster/John Knox, 2001), 168.
5. Leslie Nielsen in *Naked Gun 2 1/2: The Smell of Fear* (Paramount, 1991).
6. Tony W. Cartledge, *Vows in the Hebrew Bible and the Ancient Near East* (Sheffield, England: Sheffield Academic Press, 1992), 30.
7. http://www.creditcards.com/credit-card-news/credit-card-industry-facts-personal-debt-statistics-1276.php
8. "Johann Sebastian Bach: The Fifth Evangelist," www.christianitytoday.com/history/special/131christians/bach.html
9. Ibid.
10. Jaroslav Pelikan, *Fools for Christ* (Eugene, Oreg.: Wipf and Stock, 1955), 155.

Chapter 8: Inbox (1)

1. Art Hoppe, quoted in Rosemarie Jarski, *Words from the Wise: Over 6,000 of the Smartest Things Ever Said* (New York: Skyhorse, 2007), 215.
2. John R. W. Stott, *Your Mind Matters* (Downers Grove, Ill.: InterVarsity, 1972), 60.
3. Jonathan Edwards, *The Works of President Edwards* (New York: Carvill, 1830), 283.
4. A. W. Tozer, *Worship: The Missing Jewel* (Camp Hill, Pa.: Christian Publications, 1992), 25.
5. Dietrich Bonhoeffer, quoted in Richard J. Foster, *Celebration of Discipline* (1978; repr. San Francisco: HarperSanFrancisco, 1998), 19.
6. John C. Kricher, Gordon Morrison, and Roger Tory Peterson, *A Field Guide to Eastern Forests: North America* (New York: Houghton Mifflin, 1998), 196.
7. *Dictionary of Quotations in Communications*, comp. Lilless McPherson Shilling and Linda K. Fuller (Westport, Conn.: Greenwood, 1997), 135.
8. R. T. France, *I Came to Set the Earth on Fire* (Downers Grove, Ill.: InterVarsity, 1976), 50.
9. Michael J. Wilkins, *Following the Master: A Biblical Theology of Discipleship* (Grand Rapids: Zondervan, 1992), 74.
10. John Bracy, *Ba Gua: Advanced Hidden Knowledge in the Taoist Internal Martial Art* (Berkeley, Calif.: North Atlantic Books, 1998), 123.
11. George Barna, quoted in Greg Ogden, *Transforming Discipleship* (Downers Grove, Ill.: InterVarsity, 2003), 27.
12. Ibid.
13. Dietrich Bonhoeffer, *The Cost of Discipleship* (1948; repr., Minneapolis: Augsburg Fortress, 2000), 59.

Chapter 9: Cardboard Crosses

1. Willis Mason West, *The Ancient World from the Earliest Times to 800 A.D.*, rev. ed. (Boston: Allyn and Bacon, 1913), 51.
2. Richard Foster, *Celebration of Discipline* (San Francisco: HarperSanFrancisco, 1998), 115.
3. J. I. Packer, *Knowing God* (Downers Grove, Ill.: InterVarsity, 1973), 86.
4. Tom Hanks in *Cast Away*, directed by Robert Zemeckis, written by William Broyles Jr. (Twentieth Century Fox and DreamWorks, 2000).
5. William Gurnall, rev. by John Campbell, *The Christian in Complete Armor* (London: William Tegg, 1862), 5.
6. Axel Munthe, *The Story of San Michele* (New York: E. P. Dutton, 1934), 436.
7. Saint Augustine, quoted in John Christopher Thomas, *Footwashing in John 13 and the Johannine Community* (Edinburgh, Scotland: T. & T. Clark, 2004), 131.

Chapter 10: Feng Shui Faith

1. Napoleon Bonaparte, quoted in John S. C. Abbott, *The History of Napoleon Bonaparte*, vol. 2 (New York: Harper & Brothers, 1855), 618, 613.
2. Donna Schaper and Carole Ann Camp, *Labyrinths from the Outside In: Walking to Spiritual Insight* (Woodstock, Vt.: Skylight Paths, 2000), 2.
3. Ibid., 4.

4. Helen Raphael Sands, *The Healing Labyrinth* (New York: Gaia Books, 2001), 30, 28, 33.
5. For more information on Finger Labyrinth Designs, go to www.relax4life.com
6. For more information on portable labyrinths, see Sands, *The Healing Labyrinth*. For labyrinths located across America, see Schaper and Camp, *Labyrinths from the Outside In*, Appendix B.
7. Lauren Artress, *Walking a Sacred Path* (New York: Riverhead Books, 1995), 29–30.
8. C. S. Lewis, quoted in Walter Hooper, *C. S. Lewis: A Complete Guide to His Life and Works* (New York: HarperOne, 1998), 382.
9. Schaper and Camp, *Labyrinths from the Outside In*, 8.
10. Allan P. Ross, professor of divinity at Beeson Divinity School, Birmingham, Alabama, who teaches Hebrew exegesis.
11. Rick and Bubba host a syndicated program broadcast on FM radio; see and hear via a live feed at www.rickandbubba.com
12. Fox News, "Solar System Like Ours Found 5,000 Light Years Away," by Robert Roy Britt, February 18, 2008, http://www.foxnews.com/story/0,2933,330814,00.html#
13. *Hubblecast HD*, Number 14, March 19, 2008.
14. Henri J. M. Nouwen, Michael J. Christensen, and Rebecca Laird, *Spiritual Direction* (New York: HarperCollins, 2006), 148–49.

Chapter 11: G-Force

1. Dr. Robert Smith, Jr., associate professor of divinity, Beeson Divinity School, Birmingham, Alabama. He told me this prior to my sermon, "Holding the Hem," in May 2008. He was referring to me, not America.
2. Philip Jenkins, professor of history and religious studies, Pennsylvania State University. From his discussion at a lunch question-and-answer session at Philip Jenkins Lectures, Beeson Divinity School, Birmingham, Alabama, March 11, 2008.
3. "Are You Washed in the Blood?" by Elisha A. Hoffman, *Inspiring Hymns*, comp. Alfred B. Smith (n.p., Singspiration, 1952), 95.
4. Brother Lawrence, *The Practice of the Presence of God: Being Conversations and Letters of Nicholas Herman of Lorraine, 1895* (Westwood, N.J.: Revell, 1958), 6.
5. Ibid.
6. Brother Lawrence, quoted in Fred Raynaud, *Reflections from the Kitchen* (n.l.: PageFree Publishing, 2006), 12.
7. Eric Liddell, quoted in *Chariots of Fire*, screenplay by Colin Welland (won Academy Award for best screenplay written directly for the screen), directed by Hugh Hudson, (Enigma/Twentieth Century Fox, 1981).
8. Jonathan Edwards, *The Works of President Edwards in Four Volumes with Valuable Additions and a Copious General Index, and A Complete Index of Scripture Texts*, vol. 4 (New York: Robert Carter and Brothers, 1879), 675.
9. Martin Luther King Jr., *Why We Can't Wait* (New York: Signet Classics, 2000), 51.
10. Benedict, *St. Benedict's Rule for Monasteries*, trans. Leonard J. Doyle (Collegeville, Minn.: Liturgical Press, 1948), 42.
11. Johannes Jörgensen, *Saint Francis of Assisi*, trans. T. O'Conor Sloane (New York: Longmans, Green, 1912), 132.

12. *1,600 Quotes & Pieces of Wisdom That Just Might Help You Out When You're Stuck in a Moment and Can't Get Out of It*, comp. Gary Guthrie (Bloomington, Ind.: iUniverse, 2003), 12.
13. Martyn Lloyd-Jones, *Preaching and Preachers*, rev. ed. (London: Hodder Headline, 1998), 193.
14. Jonathan Edwards, *A Treatise Concerning Religious Affections, in Three Parts* (Philadelphia: James Crissy, G. Goodman, printer, 1821), x.

Epilogue: (NaCl)

Joe Church, quoted in "Young, Restless, and Ready for Revival" by Becky Tirabassi in *Christianity Today*, December 2007.

Acknowledgments

• • •

Acknowledgments \ak-näl-ij-mənts\

Rebecca, my best friend and Inkling

Dad, my hero
Mom, my inspiration
Pops and Mops, for great food and fun

J. I. Packer, for your convictions
Chuck Colson, for your example
Steve Holmes and Ian Bradley, doctoral supervisors

Jack Hunter, who is caught by the Catcher
Michael Bagdanovich, whom I never met, but have come to love

Atoosa Nowrouzi, woman of God
Tyson and Marge, for adventures we've had, and those still to come
Nic, Stephanie, and Andrew Francis, for figuring out what the nickel's for
Cary Hughes, encourager
Sara Beth Geoghegan, artist and singer
Brandon Mathis, www.brandon@imathis.com
Joy Mathis, prayer warrior
Steve Prokop, guitar hero
Stan, Nancy, and Hayden Elizabeth, for letting me write on your porch
Morag Scanlon, for calling the ambulance
Graham Hill, who braved the Greek transvestite

Greg Johnson, literary agent and friend
My Moody team: Greg, Lori, Holly, Jim, Tracey and Esther.

My New Orleans haunts: NOBTS, Casey's Snowballs, Commander's, and Café du Monde
And of course, my C. H. Spurgeon Facebook Group

Soli Deo Gloria

≈